PRAISE FOR *DRUCKER & ME*

"I personally witnessed this fascinating backstory between two of my best friends, Peter Drucker and Bob Buford. Now everyone can benefit from the amazing conversations Bob had with one of the brightest minds of all time."

Dr. Rick Warren
*Founding Pastor of Saddleback Church and
Author of* The Purpose Driven Life

"I loved *Drucker & Me*. I can't think of two more influential people, not only in my life but in the lives of many others, than Peter Drucker and Bob Buford. Learning from their friendship and stimulating interactions is a gift you won't want to miss!"

Ken Blanchard
Coauthor of The One Minute Manager® *and*
Leading at a Higher Level

"Only Bob Buford could capture the essence of Peter Drucker in such a moving and authentic way, for who was as close to Peter as Bob Buford? Bob's book is pure Peter."

Frances Hesselbein
*President and CEO of the Frances Hesselbein
Leadership Institute (Originally the Peter F. Drucker
Foundation for Nonprofit Management)*

"In addition to being a terrific read, *Drucker & Me* provides an intimate portrait of Peter Drucker as we've never seen him before: as a close friend and mentor. In this way, it reveals not only important organizational lessons but also wonderful life lessons. There are lots of Drucker books out there at this point, but this one is a true standout."

Rick Wartzman

Executive Director of the Drucker Institute and Columnist for Time.com

"A remarkable friendship is revealed in a compelling, inspirational, and challenging way, and the reader becomes part of this special relationship."

Steve Reinemund

Dean of Wake Forest School of Business and Retired Chairman and CEO of PepsiCo

"A mentor is a person who multiplies his or her impact by investing in the lives and work of others. Peter Drucker was such a mentor to Bob Buford and then Bob became a mentor to countless others. This is the heartwarming story of how two men changed each others' lives and then leveraged that transformation to meet 'human needs and alleviate suffering' through a chain reaction that is still changing our world."

Richard Stearns

President of World Vision US and Author of The Hole in Our Gospel *and* Unfinished

"*Drucker & Me* is absolutely outstanding. I read it once, took notes, and have returned twice again. I am delighted to be able to publicly recognize Bob and this fine work. This little book punches well above its weight! Imbued with wisdom, it is a powerful story of profound collaboration and inspired leadership, teaching us all how to lead more useful lives in service of others."

Tom Tierney
Chairman and Cofounder of the Bridgespan Group

"I did not know Peter Drucker personally yet have admired his work from a distance since as far as I can remember. *Drucker & Me* provides a perspective on this important man that few would have of any man—one that even further enhances our collective view of his incredible contributions to our work here. I am grateful for Bob's effort in sharing this with all of us."

Curt Pullen
Executive Vice President and President of Herman Miller North America and Chairman of the Board of Advisors for the Drucker Institute

"*Drucker & Me* is a wonderful example of what mentoring is supposed to be. The story is a warm relationship between mentor and his pupil. It is a model for anyone who is in a mentoring relationship and demonstrates how both people benefit from it. I felt I was part of the conversation. A bonus was the wisdom that Peter Drucker imparted that is valuable to all of us. It is worth rereading regularly. One of the best books I have read in recent years."

Wally Hawley
Cofounder of InterWest Partners and Philanthropist

"This inspiring story of an entrepreneur's collaboration with the legendary management thinker Peter Drucker shows that great ideas combined with passionate execution really can change the world."

Mike Ullman
Chief Executive Officer and Director of J. C. Penney

"Bob Buford creates another great book—and as an extra benefit we get the perceptive wisdom of Peter Drucker added to the mix as well."

Philip Anschutz
CEO and Owner of The Anschutz Company and Philanthropist

"Peter Drucker rarely wrote forewords to books by other authors. Yet he did it twice for Bob Buford. That gives you an idea of the mutual respect Drucker and Buford had for each other. Their relationship comes alive in *Drucker & Me*, and in the process we learn much about the lives of both men that can be a beacon for our self-development."

Bruce Rosenstein
Managing Editor of Leader to Leader *and author of* Create Your Future the Peter Drucker Way

"What an extraordinary story—the life partnership between Bob Buford, the world's most brilliant entrepreneur for faith, and Peter Drucker, the leading management thinker of the last century—and how it has changed the world!"

Bill Drayton
CEO of Ashoka: Innovators for the Public

"I have been an admirer of Bob Buford's life-changing books for many years. *Drucker & Me* is my new favorite. The book is very engaging and skillfully personalizes the relationship between Bob and Peter Drucker, providing unique and wonderful insights on Drucker as a man and a friend."

Jack Bergstrand
CEO, Brand Velocity, Inc.

"*Drucker & Me* is about the power of partnership: Peter Drucker's genius joined to Bob Buford's receptive, entrepreneurial energy. Until now, few people have realized this synergistic relationship literally changed the face of today's church. A book filled with great insights any spiritual leader can benefit from, this is a story that needs to be told."

Robert Lewis
Pastor, Founder of Men's Fraternity

See the back of the book for . . .
More Insights from Readers and Friends of Peter and Bob

DRUCKER
& Me

DRUCKER
&Me

**What a Texas Entrepreneur Learned
from the Father of Modern Management**

BOB BUFORD

WORTHY*
PUBLISHING

Library of Congress Control Number: 2013954256

For foreign and subsidiary rights, contact rights@worthypublishing.com

Published in association with Derek Bell, Mosaic Trust, LLC

ISBN: 978-1-68397-019-4 (trade paper)

Cover Design: Christopher Tobias, Tobias' Outerwear for Books
Interior Design: Susan Browne Design

Printed in the United States of America

> "The best way to predict
> the future is to create it."
> —Peter F. Drucker

To the legacy of Peter F. Drucker,
who helped so many of us
on our journey, and to those who
continue to press on.

CONTENTS

FOREWORD

THIS IS A wonderful little book by one of Peter Drucker's very best students. Bob Buford tells the story of reaching out to Drucker, learning directly from the master himself, and how he applied what he learned to change lives. It is exceptionally well-written and provides a glimpse into the secret sauce of how a truly great teacher can have an impact on the world through a truly great student. Bob laces together a short biography of Drucker with Bob's own personal autobiography, while also sharing some of Drucker's most important lessons and observations in an incisive way.

Peter Drucker was a prolific genius. He published in excess of ten thousand pages across hundreds of articles and more than thirty books, packed with astute observations and penetrating insights. Thoughtful leaders know that they *should* engage with Drucker's ideas, but the sheer overwhelming volume creates a significant practical problem: where to begin, and how best to access his teachings? If you have not yet jumped into the vast ocean of Drucker's ideas, this would be a superb starting point. And if you have read Drucker, this book adds a unique perspective; if you've ever wondered what it would be like to have Peter Drucker as a personal teacher and mentor, this memoir gives a rare and authentic glimpse of that experience.

> Thoughtful leaders know that they should engage with Drucker's ideas, but the sheer overwhelming volume creates a significant practical problem: where to begin, and how best to access his teachings? If you have not yet jumped into the vast ocean of Drucker's ideas, this would be a superb starting point.

As I enjoyed reading Bob's engaging story, I noted three primary elements of Peter's teaching impact. *First, he pushed his students to think* for *themselves, rather than simply telling them what to think.* Peter would ask Bob to write a long letter to him prior to their annual meetings, forcing Bob to think rigorously about the challenges he faced. Then, Peter would begin his teaching sessions by pushing and challenging not with points and ideas, but with questions. Peter's greatest teaching came not in giving answers, but by pushing and challenging with the right questions. He wanted Bob to think for himself. And because he taught like Socrates, Peter learned at least as much from his students as his students learned from him, a secret to his own continuous self-renewal. The greatest teachers begin with humility, a belief that only by first learning from their students can they be of greatest service to them.

Second, Peter changed not just the minds of his students but their lives and, through them, the lives of other people. Think of a student like a vector heading out into time and space; if you can change the trajectory of that vector even a little bit, those small changes will turn into a large sweeping arc years down the road. And then if that vector in turn changes the trajectory of tens or hundreds or thousands of other vectors, then a teacher can have a multiplicative impact on the world. This is exactly what Drucker-as-teacher did. He changed student lives partly by setting audacious standards for the best students, such as challenging Bob to make his second half of life more significant than his first half, obliterating any desire Bob might have for retirement. Drucker challenged Bob to "transform the latent energy of American Christianity into active energy"—no small task—and thereby launched Bob on a quest that would consume his most creative and productive years.

Third, Peter got a high "Return on Luck" with the right students. I've become fascinated with the question of luck, and its role (or lack thereof) for those who achieve exceptional

results. It turns out that when we rigorously defined and quan-
tified luck, the best-performing leaders and their companies
were *not* luckier—they did not get more good luck, less bad
luck, better timing of luck, or bigger spikes of luck than the
less-successful comparison cases in our research. However,
they *did* achieve a higher *return* on luck. They took whatever
luck events they got, whether good luck or bad luck, recognized them, seized them, and made more out of them than
others. The question for all of us is not whether we will get
luck, but what will we do with the luck that we get. How does
this relate to Peter Drucker? Think of it this way: For a teacher,
one of the most important luck events is when a great student
crosses your path; then upon recognizing when he or she is
blessed by the unexpected arrival of a great student, a great
teacher invests 10x in that student. Peter Drucker realized
that a significant teaching investment in Bob Buford would
yield a return far in excess of investing in the average student.

Drucker's impact derives not just from his ideas, but from
his entire approach to ideas, and ultimately his power as a
teacher. Drucker was deeply empirical; he derived insights
not by pure theory, but by looking at actual facts and building
a theory based on facts, evidence, and practicality. Once when
I asked Drucker the purpose of his consulting, he said, "Ah,
that is my laboratory." He didn't just want to sit around and

think big thoughts; he wanted to derive insights that would have a tangible impact on people's lives. Yet, while Drucker focused on tangible results, he elevated his teachings to a frame much larger than "how-to" mechanics. "He diverted my attention from the nuts and bolts of running a business," writes Bob in these pages, "and focused instead on the broader horizons of things such as character, vision, and responsibility." Drucker saw management—and its sibling, leadership—as a liberal art, not a technocratic exercise.

> Drucker's impact derives not just from his ideas, but from his entire approach to ideas, and ultimately his power as a teacher.

I believe that Drucker's work was guided by one audacious overarching question: What does it take—what principles are needed—to make society both more productive *and* more humane? Bob Buford once told me that he believed Peter Drucker contributed as much to the triumph of freedom over totalitarianism as anyone, including Winston Churchill. At first, I was puzzled by Bob's rather extreme statement, but then came to understand and appreciate that he might well be right. For free society to function at its best—and to thereby compete with tyranny—we must have high-performing, freely-operating organizations spread throughout society; these autonomous institutions, in turn, depend on having excellent management. This is a classic Druckerian duality, linking together big and small, practical and philosophical, micro and macro; on the one hand, he stayed grounded in "what works" for managers, and on the other hand, he framed "what works" in the context of one of the most important long-term questions that human societies must address.

Finally, and most important, Drucker infused all of his work with the great compassion and concern for the individual, and this is the cornerstone of what made him a great teacher. I do indeed believe that Drucker's body of work is essentially right, that his insights about the workings of the social world have been—and will continue to be—proved right by history. But there is one place where I believe Peter Drucker got it wrong, at least in part. When Bob Buford asked what could be done to advance Peter's legacy, Drucker impatiently waved the question away: "My legacy is my writing." True, but incomplete. An equally significant legacy, in my view, may be found in his students, and their impact on the world. If Drucker had not been such a great teacher, if he had closeted himself like a hermit with a typewriter, I believe his impact would have been profoundly stunted. And there is no better testament to that aspect of Peter's legacy than this gift from Bob Buford, *Drucker & Me*.

Jim Collins
Boulder, Colorado
April 8, 2013

INTRODUCTION

WHEN I BEGAN working on this book, I pulled a team of creative people together—as I often do when starting a new project—to help me give the story its shape and focus. In addition to more than twenty years of friendship with best-selling author and management consultant Peter F. Drucker, I also had transcripts of practically every meeting I had that included Peter—more than a thousand pages in all. I suspected there was a book hiding somewhere in all of this information, but I needed some objective eyes and ears to help me find it.

That process took close to five years. My team would meet for a day or so and think we had just the right book, but when I started writing, it felt like just another book about Peter Drucker—of which there are and will continue to be many. The last thing I wanted to do was write "just another."

Finally, after several false starts, one of the members of my team said something like, "You had the fortune of seeing Peter up close and personal. He was your friend. Why don't you just write about your friend. Let us see Peter from this intimate vantage point."

Which is exactly what I attempt to do in this book—reveal the man behind the legend.

Typically, books like this gain a hearing because of the dirt they dish up. If that's what you were hoping for, I'm afraid you'll be disappointed. First, I have no respect for "friends" who exploit a relationship in such a crass and disingenuous fashion, and I am not about to lose my self-respect.

But even if in a momentary lapse of judgment I decided to "tell all," I would fail miserably in that genre for the simple reason that there's nothing to tell. Peter was one of those rare individuals who really did practice what he preached. His motivation for all that he did professionally was to contribute toward a "fully functioning society," and for Peter that began with a fully functioning human being. He lived a principled life, uncluttered by unwholesome pursuits or frivolous diversions. He loved his wife, his family, and his work. If he had any time left over from those affections, it probably meant he wasn't spending enough time on them.

In terms of friendship, we were an unlikely pairing. A generation apart in age. One of us spoke English with a heavy Austrian accent. The other spoke Texan. I owned a cable television company. Peter didn't even own a television. I wore a business suit. Peter wore a long-sleeve shirt buttoned at the top with a bolo tie in place of a necktie. I followed the Dallas

Cowboys. He followed Japanese art. But as we would both learn a few years into our relationship, we shared a passion for a phenomenon that could literally change the world.

> Peter was one of those rare individuals who really did practice what he preached. His motivation for all that he did professionally was to contribute toward a "fully functioning society," and for Peter that began with a fully functioning human being.

At one of the final meetings of my creative team, we spent some time brainstorming an appropriate title for this book, fully knowing that publishers seldom use titles suggested by authors. But having a title in mind tends to help keep you focused on the task at hand. One of the titles on our list that eventually did not make our cut was *Saving Society*. As noble, ambitious, and perhaps arrogant as this sounds, it describes what both Peter and I felt we were called to do, and in this book I will do my best to accurately explain how we planned to do it.

Bob Buford

1

YOU MAY GO NOW

"This time he's not coming back."

—DORIS DRUCKER

HOW MANY TIMES had I heard him say, "Begin with the end in sight"? A dozen? A hundred? It was one of those maxims I applied to just about every project I undertook, so it is fitting that I apply it here, which is to say this story begins in Aspen, Colorado, where I retreat from time to time to think, write, and recalibrate. On this particular occasion I had invited Brett Eastman, a very creative thinker, to join me. The two of us were deep into something that at the time seemed enormously important when my wife, Linda, interrupted us with news I had always known would come some day.

My dear friend and mentor, Peter F. Drucker, was dying.

The details punctuated this unwelcome message like an intruder in the middle of the night: He had not been feeling well and was taken to the hospital. Family members were flying in from all over the world to say farewell. There was talk about removing him from life support.

I knew what I had to do, but for many reasons didn't want

to do it. Even as he crept past ninety, Peter remained as intellectually sharp as ever, and I could not imagine him any other way. I also knew him well enough to know he would not have been pleased to be the object of any sentimental hand-wringing, especially if he could not defend himself with a clever admonishment to those who had gathered to say good-bye.

Then there were the logistics of getting there, complicated by Peter's brutal objectivity and Old World practicality. It's never easy getting from Aspen to anywhere quickly, but finding Pomona County Hospital dampened my already limited enthusiasm for negotiating the Los Angeles freeway system. Peter, who seemed to know a lot about nearly everything, once told me that a good regional hospital will take care of you as well as the Mayo Clinic or UCLA Medical Center, and I had to smile when I learned where he had chosen to spend what may have been his final days.

I also am of the opinion that if there are things left unsaid between friends in a situation such as this, then it wasn't much of a relationship to begin with. Neither of us needed a deathbed to prompt kindness or appreciation out of us. What gain could possibly come from the awkwardness both of us would most certainly feel? Yet any thought of staying in Aspen quickly evaporated by a simple declaration from Linda.

"You have to go."

Of course she was right—she almost always is—and when Brett offered to travel with me, I somewhat reluctantly began to pack as he worked his cellphone to line up our flights. Even as Linda drove us to Aspen's tiny Pitkin County Airport, I retreated into a silent reverie of sadness seasoned with a fair amount of dread. Other than Linda and Jesus, through his words and example in the Bible, no one has had more of an influence on me than Peter, and this could easily be the last time I would see him alive.

Brett somehow stitched together flights that got us to Long Beach. I rented a car as he left to rejoin his family in Orange County, and since it had been an awfully long day of travel, I checked into a rather drab hotel along I-10, double-locked my door, and tried to get some sleep. Between the noise from the freeway outside my window, an unsettling pounding on my door in the middle of the night, and recurring flashbacks of the many good times I had spent with Peter—to say nothing of the lingering thought of having to see him under such terrible circumstances—sleep came in small doses.

When I got to his room, he was all alone, connected by wires and tubes to a variety of devices that either monitored his condition or kept him breathing. Over the years we may have met more than a hundred times, yet this was unlike any meeting I had had with Peter. Instead of the usual conversation characterized by his meandering answers to my questions that always looped back to an answer made profound by its obvious simplicity, we actually spoke very little. Fully alert and gracious as ever, he was clearly in a bad way, and I was glad I had come. Normally, before we met I would send him a long, rambling letter that served as our agenda, but today, my only purpose was to be there.

> Over the years we may have met more than a hundred times, yet this was unlike any meeting I had had with Peter.

After about a half hour, he abruptly brought our conversation to an end.

"Well, you've done what you've come here to do, so you may go now."

It was so typically Peter. He fully understood why I was there and after giving me the gift of one final meeting to say whatever needed to be said, he released me from my assignment. I honestly cannot recall precisely what we said to each

other, but it didn't seem to matter. It was an almost word-
less summary of a twenty-plus year relationship between two
friends who knew exactly what was going on and did not want
to belabor the issue.

And so I left with a mixture of sadness and gratitude. Sadness at the almost certain belief that I would never see him
again—at least not in this world—but gratitude for having been
so deeply influenced by this great man. I left his room, walked to
my car, drove to the airport, and flew back to Aspen and waited
for the inevitable, only to enjoy one more surprise from Peter.

To everyone's amazement, he recovered. Though physically quite frail, he was able to return home.

"I AM A WRITER"

Fast forward several months to September 29, 2005. Whenever I visited Peter, I always tried to take someone along with
me. I felt it was almost selfish not to share with someone what
I would undoubtedly gain from any meeting with him. On this
particular occasion, I had asked Derek Bell, a very bright
young consultant who had served in a temporary leadership
role with the Drucker Institute, to join me at Peter's home
on Wellesly Drive in Claremont, California. We had what we
thought was a grand agenda, and that was to talk with Peter

about his legacy—especially all of his writing—and how we might help him with that. Between Derek's past experience in publishing and my business acumen (honed by Peter), we had some ideas about how Peter's ideas, writing, and influence could best be kept alive for future generations.

When Derek and I walked into his modest living room, it was obvious that Peter was failing. His wife, Doris, had confided to us that he spent most of his days sleeping and that she had to practically douse him with water to get him ready to meet us. But she also assured me that especially in his later years when his health had begun to deteriorate, my visits had been something of a tonic for him.

As always, I made a mental note of the books on Peter's coffee table. Peter had taught me how to learn and the importance of continually aiming higher, a striving for perfection that he had picked up from the great Italian composer, Giuseppe Verdi. Every three years Peter selected a subject and then immersed himself in it. When the time was up, he moved on to something else. There lying on Peter's coffee table on this day were books about microbiology.

He greeted us warmly from his favorite chair as I settled in beside him to his right, Derek to his left, and Doris on the couch across from him. As I began to explain why we were there, Peter listened politely until I had finished and then in his inimitable style crisply ended our "discussion" of his legacy with four sentences that I remember verbatim:

"I am a writer," he began. "My legacy is my writing. I did not create an institution. Now what would you like to talk about?"

Peter listened politely until I had finished and then in his inimitable style crisply ended our "discussion" of his legacy with four sentences that I remember verbatim: "I am a writer," he began. "My legacy is my writing."

The first three of those sentences pretty much summed up his career. Peter was a great observer of humanity. In November 2001, *The Economist* commissioned the then-ninety-one-year-old to write a special twenty-seven page piece about "the next society." "Tomorrow is closer than you think," the magazine averred. "Peter Drucker explains how it will differ from today, and what needs to be done to prepare for it." He was all substance and wrote with exquisite clarity, which is probably why he was shunned by the academy. As famed management writer Tom Peters once put it: "Drucker effectively bypassed the intellectual establishment. So it's not surprising that they hated his guts." But Peter didn't care. He was not concerned that a building or institute be named after him.

It was almost as if Peter was telling us that if you must have a special meeting to plan your legacy, you really don't have one at all. He had been working on his legacy all his life, writing books that contained few footnotes because his thinking was original; he did not borrow from others but left a treasure of wisdom for all. Peter had a streak of mischief in him that he was normally able to contain, but I thought I detected a sly smile cross his face as he so deftly closed the door on this legacy business. Had he the energy, he might have nudged me and said, "So what are you doing out here, big boy?"

It turned out that Peter, on his own, had negotiated a deal with *Harvard Business Review*, giving them the publishing rights to his books whenever their original publisher declared them out of print. The elegant simplicity of the deal was classic Drucker, leaving Derek and me a bit sheepish and marvelously impressed again with his crystal clear foresight.

But even this brief exchange had taken its toll on Peter's strength. Doris, always a fierce protector of her husband of seventy-one years, signaled the end of the meeting.

"Peter! It's time for your nap." (Once, over dinner, I asked Doris what her mission in life was. She responded crisply, "The preservation of Peter Drucker.")

With her help he struggled to his feet, and with one hand on his walker, he extended his other to us.

"Bob, so nice to see you again. Mr. Bell, a pleasure to meet you."

And then he shuffled off to his bedroom, Doris at his side.

We stood in the living room until Doris returned. I let my eyes take in his beloved Japanese prints on the wall across from me and tried to recall the very first time I had knocked on the door to this house. In many ways, nothing had changed inside that humble home. Yet so much had been accomplished as a result of that unlikely first encounter with a man I once had known only through his writing.

After making sure Peter was cared for, Doris walked us to the front door. Never one to be sentimental, she pulled me aside and gave it to me straight.

"This time he's not coming back."

I stepped out into the warm California sun and paused before getting into the rental car. Some of my fondest memories traced their way back to this small house. I smiled to myself as I recalled my youthful chutzpah in assuming that the man who advised the CEOs of Intel and Procter & Gamble would take me on as a client. I almost laughed at the incongruity of this Old World European gentleman hanging out with a disparate group of mavericks to which I had introduced him. It had all started here, and I knew this time that it was about to end. But that it wouldn't really. Because

Peter had already settled the question of his legacy. That was Peter—a step ahead of all of us.

Two months later, Peter F. Drucker, my friend and mentor, died.

And this is the rest of the story.

2
BEWARE THE MAN ON THE WHITE HORSE

"No century has seen more leaders with more charisma than the Twentieth Century, and never have political leaders done greater damage than the four giant leaders of the Twentieth Century: Stalin, Mussolini, Hitler and Mao."

—PETER DRUCKER

AS WELL AS I thought I knew Peter, it wasn't until the obituaries started appearing that I learned about his earlier years. From these as well as other accounts, it seemed clear to me that in many ways, he was born at the right time in the right place.

Vienna in 1909 was widely recognized as the intellectual hub of Europe, if not the world. And Peter's parents, Caroline and Adolph, a top trade official for the Austro-Hungarian Empire, traveled easily among the elites of the day. Indeed, their home on Kaasgrabengasse, a quiet avenue in the Viennese neighborhood of Döbling, embodied the tradition of the European salon society. Two or three times a week his parents hosted gatherings of state officials, doctors, scientists, musicians, and writers to discuss a remarkably wide range of topics. Peter, who would become a true polymath, soaked in all of it.

Among his parents' contemporaries was Sigmund Freud, who became known as the "father of psychoanalysis." Peter was eight years old when he first met Freud and recalled what his father told him later that afternoon: "Remember, today you have just met the most important man in Austria and perhaps in Europe." Ironically, Peter would go on to be celebrated as the "father of modern management," a title that held little interest or fondness for him.

At age eighteen, Peter left Austria for Germany, where he enrolled at the University of Frankfurt to study law. If his privileged childhood nurtured his longstanding intellectual curiosity, his years in Germany fostered an ongoing suspicion of power, thanks to another Austrian-born citizen who was beginning to make his mark in Germany: Adolf Hitler.

The year was 1927, seven years after Hitler convinced the German Workers Party to change its name to the National Socialist German Workers Party (NSDAP), later nicknamed the Nazi Party. Ever since Hitler had been sent to spy on the German Workers Party in 1919, his charisma and skill as an orator had fueled his—and his party's—rise. Such was his appeal that the NSDAP grew from a mere twenty-five members in 1919 to more than two thousand in 1920. By 1921, Hitler ousted Anton Drexler to become the head of the party, and over the next several years Hitler would foment dissent against the German government, spend a year in prison where he wrote *Mein Kampf*, and then begin a systematic and strong-armed campaign to become, at age forty-three, the Chancellor.

Peter arrived in Frankfurt around the same time Hitler held his first Nazi meeting in Berlin. To support himself, Peter worked as a trainee in a brokerage firm. As the Great Depression set in, he watched with increasing alarm as Hitler and his propaganda machine consolidated power. Peter recognized the threat brought by a charismatic "savior" seeking to build a strong, centralized government by appealing to the fears of a nation in economic and social chaos.

> Peter arrived in Frankfurt around the same time Hitler held his first Nazi meeting in Berlin. . . . Peter recognized the threat brought by a charismatic "savior."

It was also during this time that Peter demonstrated his skill as a journalist, eventually becoming an editor at the half-million circulation daily newspaper, the *Frankfurter General-Anzeiger*. His primary responsibility at the newspaper was to cover foreign affairs and economics, but he often attended the mass political rallies in Frankfurt and covered Hitler when he visited the city. While many of his contemporaries dismissed Hitler as a radical on the fringes of politics, Peter took him seriously. And once the Nazis gained a foothold, they apparently began to take Peter seriously as well. In 1933 he published a pamphlet on Friedrich Julius Stahl, a leading German conservative philosopher, which so offended the Nazis they publicly burned it. Perhaps foreshadowing his tenacious conviction for doing what was right, four years later he published another pamphlet, *Die Judenfrage in Deutchland (The Jewish Question in Germany)*, which was similarly received by the Nazis.

Shortly after his second pamphlet was banned, Peter moved to London, and by 1937 he had immigrated to the United States. But his brief time in Germany helped shape his thinking about management because, as he later reflected, unless all sectors of society work effectively, tyranny is sure to fill the void. "To make our institutions perform responsibly, autonomously, and on a high level of achievement is thus the only safeguard of freedom and dignity in the pluralistic society of institutions," he once wrote. "Performing, responsible management is the alternative to tyranny and our only protection against it."

MANAGING TO LIVE

To think of Peter only in the context of "management" would be to miss the point of his real contribution to society. Peter himself tended to reject the labels others used to describe him and thought of himself more as a writer than anything else. In his early academic career he taught politics and philosophy at Bennington College in Vermont. A few years later, in 1943, he began a systematic study of General Motors, which led to the publication of his landmark book, *Concept of the Corporation*. He then moved to New York University's Graduate School of Business and shortly thereafter heard a fellow Austrian, the economist Joseph Schumpeter, say something that would change the trajectory of his life: "I know it is not enough to be remembered for books and theories. One does not make a difference unless it is a difference in people's lives."

This is really what Peter was all about: making a difference. He always had the bigger picture in mind even though his particular milieu was the world of business. "None of our institutions exists by itself and is an end in itself," he wrote in his book *Management*. "Every one is an organ of society and exists for the sake of society. Business is no exception. Free enterprise cannot be justified as being good for business; it can be justified only as being good for society."

While he was intensely interested in management as a profession, he believed that corporations—fast emerging as perhaps our most important institutions—had to be effective and responsible if we were to have a functioning society. The failure of Germany's institutions in the 1930s opened the door to a charismatic leader who promised to fix society. "Beware the man on the white horse," Peter used to warn. He had seen firsthand the damage these saviors can inflict on a society in decline: "No century has seen more leaders with more charisma than the Twentieth Century, and never have political leaders done greater damage than the four giant leaders of the Twentieth Century: Stalin, Mussolini, Hitler and Mao," he declared in *The New Realities*.

While he was intensely interested in management as a profession, he believed that corporations— fast emerging as perhaps our most important institutions—had to be effective and responsible if we were to have a functioning society.

The best way to inoculate against such destruction, according to Peter, is to help people get the best out of themselves for their own benefit as well as the benefit of others. Management just happened to be the discipline he chose in which to do that. Interestingly, his most famous text, *The Practice of Management*, was not so much a strategic career move but was characteristically written to meet a need. There were plenty of books out there at the time on individual aspects of running a business—finance, for example, or human resources. Each of them "reminded me of a book on human anatomy that would discuss one joint in the body—the elbow, for instance— without even mentioning the arm, let alone the skeleton and musculature," Drucker later recalled. *The Practice of Management* was the first that put it all together. The book laid the foundation for the discipline of management and propelled Peter into a career that would include teaching, writing, and consulting.

After twenty-one years at New York University, Peter moved to California to become professor of social sciences and management at Claremont Graduate School. He continued his prolific writing career and advised a host of companies that included General Electric, Procter & Gamble, Coca-Cola, and a small, family-owned business headquartered in Tyler, Texas . . . Buford Television Inc.

3

FIRST ENCOUNTER

"Drucker's primary contribution is not a single idea, but rather an entire body of work that has one gigantic advantage: nearly all of it is essentially right. Drucker has an uncanny ability to develop insights about the workings of the social world, and to later be proved right by history."

—JIM COLLINS

AS I CHECKED one last time in the mirror and grabbed my attaché case, I felt something like Dorothy and the Tin Man preparing to approach the green castle of the Wizard of Oz. Only Peter Drucker was the real thing—not a little man behind a curtain. As it turned out, he was more real than I could have imagined.

I walked from Griswold's, a fraying and in-need-of-much-repair-that-never-came, faux California Spanish low-rise hotel splayed over a generously landscaped site four blocks from Peter's home. The weather was balmy California, but I was fully decked out for this occasion in my best fall-weight wool herringbone suit, a paisley tie pulled carefully and not too comfortably into place. I was forty-two years old.

As a young man, the full weight of managing a family business had descended on my shoulders ten years earlier. My mother, the pioneering founder of a television broadcast company, had met death in a hotel fire. The blaze, as it turned out, was confined to only one room at the Fairmont Hotel in Dallas, the result of a chafing dish igniting overnight. I was told of her death by a deputy sheriff at my front door.

I was the oldest of three sons, and from that time on, I was the oldest family member. I was determined to become wealthy in the broadcasting business where the rising tide of America's insatiable appetite for television was lifting many a boat, mine included.

My objective, starting from a small base, was to outgrow in percentage terms all the public companies in this business. That's pretty much what happened. Beginning in 1971, the year of my mother's death, my company's market value grew at more than 25 percent annually for a dozen years—very heady times for a young CEO. I read not long ago that only 1 percent of companies grow at more than 15 percent a year for a full decade. I was very determined and very fortunate.

But that's getting ahead of the story. Walking that morning

in the clear air (clearer then than now), I could see why people move to California. The weather was motion-picture-level beautiful. The yards were landscaped way beyond what the Texas heat would tolerate. There was a sense of pride in those lawns and gardens. I was eager and filled with anticipation.

INTELLECTUAL SOUL MATE

My admiration for Peter Drucker rested entirely on his ideas. As a young and naive manager, I had read everything I could get my hands on, always looking for that edge to help us sustain our remarkable growth. Much of what I read seemed trendy—designed more to sell books than to guide behavior. (Anybody remember Robert Townsend of Avis fame?) There was also an abundance of superficial pop psychobabble on bookshelves and available for hire through seminars at the local Holiday Inn. Faddish. Here today, gone tomorrow. It was kind of like eating cotton candy at the State Fair before the Texas-Oklahoma game—an important ritual for me each October. The game had mythical status and long-remembered significance, but the cotton candy evaporated in my mouth, sticky sweet for a moment, then quickly gone.

Peter's books were different—whole orders of magnitude different. Deeply rooted in astonishing social observation, Peter towered above the rest. I had continued accumulating but long since quit reading articles in *Harvard Business Review*, except for Peter Drucker's.

Following Peter's wisdom was analogous to investing in an index fund. He wasn't always right, but he beat the market 80 percent of the time.

Peter's thinking, so highly principled, felt as solid as granite to me. He wrote from a perspective that gave me the steel girders that framed the business practice that guided me through a forest of here-today-and-gone-tomorrow concepts. Peter had authority. Gravitas. He brought insight, perspective, and context where others spoke of mechanics and calculation. And beyond that, Peter's ideas for navigating the *human* side of enterprise resonated with my heart. I was moral, but not moralistic. I was grounded in ideas, but not ideological.

> Peter's thinking, so highly principled, felt as solid as granite to me. He wrote from a perspective that gave me the steel girders that framed the business practice that guided me through a forest of here-today-and-gone-tomorrow concepts.

In Peter, I found a soul mate. He just seemed to square up on every level that was important to me: intellectual, spiritual, and practical. For example, his thoughts on wealth and money mirrored my own and were somewhat counter-cultural then (and now).

He saw money as a necessity to finance a business that grows and serves customers—not money for the sole purpose of getting rich. Even then, before anyone occupied Wall Street or called out the "1 percent," Peter found wealth for the sake of wealth obscene. While he never stated it in these terms, his view of wealth seemed to conform to biblical warnings of the seductive nature of money.

Through Peter's writing, I had begun to understand the principles that were fundamental to understanding human interaction—not just the headline stuff, but the assumptions that were at the heart of things across centuries. They became my touchstones. As my friend Jim Collins, the best-selling management writer, was later to say in the foreword to *The Daily Drucker*:

> *Drucker's primary contribution is not a single idea, but rather an entire body of work that has one gigantic advantage: nearly all of it is essentially right. Drucker has an uncanny ability to develop insights about the workings of the social world, and to later be proved right by history.*

That's *exactly* what I discovered. For the past ten years I had relentlessly sought out everything Peter had to say. The more I read, the more I recognized that his wisdom was unmatched. So I did what any forty-one-year-old from a small town in Texas running a business not quite on the scale of a General Motors or Procter & Gamble would do. I sat down and wrote a letter to this giant and asked him if he would help me with *my* business.

It never really occurred to me at the time that Peter Drucker might have bigger fish to fry, and I owe that confidence to my mother. She was a risk taker and forceful, dedicated to success in business and to raising me with the gift of self-assurance. When I was in high school she introduced me wherever we went as the "world's greatest left end." The truth was that, though I earned a starting position my senior year, I was merely adequate as a football player. Still, I loved hearing her introduce me that way, and words like that gave me affirmation and inspiration and enough chutzpah to write Peter.

So you can just imagine how I felt that sunny morning in Pasadena on my way to Peter F. Drucker's *house*. Peter's presence through writing had been almost god-like (he later warned me against this in no uncertain terms). His authority was almost scriptural for me. By that I mean there was something liberating about pushing off from my two great sources: I chose to trust the Bible for my spiritual reference and to trust Peter for my organizational reference. I therefore didn't fret about the moral and the practical rightness of these two dependable references. I could focus on execution rather than always looking over my shoulder to wonder about principles and concepts. I could focus on getting results and performance upon the platform and within the boundaries of these two sources—the spiritual/transcendent and the practical/contemporary. And what was amazing to me was that I never found the two sources to be out of sync with one another.

> His authority was almost scriptural for me. By that I mean there was something liberating about pushing off from my two great sources: I chose to trust the Bible for my spiritual reference and to trust Peter for my organizational reference.

I had heard Peter speak before in public seminars. I always imagined that if I had been Moses on sacred ground enchanted by a burning bush and listening to a thundering oracle from above, that voice would have a deep resonant tone with a European accent, just like Peter's. In the few appearances I had experienced Peter (that's the right word for it) beforehand and in all the appearances I have participated in afterward, he had a magic about him. People would sit in rapt attention, transfixed by the sheer gestalt of this man. You could hear a pin drop. People were almost afraid to breathe. And it was substance, not theatrics, that captivated us.

A HUMBLE INNER SANCTUM

At last, I was to meet this great presence in my life in person. My feeling was one of excitement and anticipation, colored by not a little bit of intimidation. It seemed almost too good to be true. Here was the one person on earth whose opinion was the most determinative to my life. I had carefully written and rewritten—eight drafts before I got it just right—a letter asking for a consulting day. I suppose I didn't really expect I would get a positive response. After all, I was the CEO of a small, private (*very* private) family business that nobody knew anything about. I was young and relatively inexperienced, asking for some help from a man sought out by Jack Welch. Peter was the seminal thinker in the field of management, respected around the world. Who was I to think he would even read my letter, let alone invite me to his home for a day?

The first surprise was that he did just that. The second was his home. I almost walked past it and certainly would not have distinguished it from the other unpretentious dwellings on the street if I hadn't had a house number. There were two midsize Japanese cars in the driveway. As I soon learned, he didn't even have an office outside a converted second bedroom inside this pleasant but unexceptional suburban ranch house.

I rang the doorbell, which clanged like a fire station inside (Peter was hard of hearing). After a brief space, I heard movement inside and a voice that said, "I'm coming. I'm coming." Outgoing mail was crammed into an oversized, fire-engine-red mailbox on the wall just beside me on a small porch. The door opened. Peter extended his hand and drew me inside with a warm, "Come in. Come in, Mr. Buford." Very European and gracious. No one ever called me "Mr. Buford" except years earlier when a vice president from the local bank called to say that I was overdrawn and could I immediately make a deposit.

But here I was. Inside the inner sanctum. Peter ushered me to a glassed-in porch toward the back of a house that looked over a small swimming pool. I sat down in a creaking circa 1950s wicker chair across from Peter, no desk interfering, and my first consulting session began with these words: "Welcome, Mr. Buford. Now what shall we talk about?"

Desperate not to waste an opportunity, I jumped right into the business at hand. Peter patiently listened, asked a lot of questions, and seemed genuinely interested in my little family enterprise. He immediately put me at ease, erasing any insecurity or sense that I had no business being there. All too soon, my time was up and Peter politely walked me to the front door and wished me well.

I almost skipped back to my hotel, high on the adrenalin rush of not just meeting a man I admired so much, but having him take an interest in my business. I could not have known then that this would mark the beginning of a relationship that would continue for the next twenty-three years. All I knew was that I had just spent a remarkable day with *the* Peter F. Drucker.

Ironically, Peter's counsel in a subsequent meeting—and my own enthusiasm to go big into what was called subscription television—led me to lose a million dollars. Generally speaking, you tend to avoid retaining consultants whose advice causes you to lose money, but I couldn't wait for our next meeting.

4

STRICTLY BUSINESS

"He normally begins about a thousand years away from the point and goes in a very wide loop that arrives at the point exactly. He uses illustrations from many disciplines to shed light on the point he is making, and each story builds on the last. He wants you to think about your situation in a larger context."

—FRED SMITH

OVER THE NEXT several years, the pattern was pretty much the same. As the date for our next meeting approached, Peter would invite me to write him a long letter describing whatever it was I wanted to talk about with him. That would serve as our agenda. I always took that assignment seriously, drafting my thoughts and ideas in longhand, revising and editing until I got it just right, before handing it off to my assistant to type— on what was known then as a typewriter—before mailing it off to Mount Olympus.

Then I would drive from Tyler to Dallas, park in one of the cavernous structures at DFW, ride the shuttle to the terminal, board my flight to the Ontario, California, airport where I rented a car, drove the twenty minutes to Griswold's Hotel, checked in, and then walked the four blocks to 636 Wellesley Drive before ringing that cacophonous doorbell. On my way I would always stop by Sherwood Florist and bring Doris a potted orchid. She had a little garden of them, and that became kind of a ritual with us.

Peter always greeted me genially, making me feel as if he actually had been looking forward to our time together—that I was his most important client. I got the same affirmation from him as I did from my mother when she bragged to everyone about my football prowess. Neither was insincere, for just as my mother believed in me more than I believed in myself, Peter treated me as if I was just as important as Jack Welch and in many ways replaced the father that I had never really known.

A CONSULTATION AND A SANDWICH

Doris always joined him in greeting me in the entryway of their home, but soon she would disappear into the house, and after kindly requesting an update on the welfare of my wife, Linda, and son, Ross, Peter would motion for me to join him in their sparsely furnished living room. He never mentioned this, but it was clear to me that his interest in me beyond my business was an example of practicing what he consistently had preached: I was a customer and foremost to him was to know and understand me—to care about me as a person—before he had any right to try and help me.

Around noon, Doris would bring us sandwiches and then duck back out of the way as we continued our conversation over lunch. A Doris-made sandwich was memorable and always the same. A piece of bread with maybe a little butter on it. Then meat of some kind, and not all that much of it. Finally, another piece of buttered bread topping it off. That was it, but it was always enough, and besides, who would have guessed that a consulting session with Peter Drucker came with a sandwich made by his wife?

Sometimes for lunch we would vary our routine and go to Rillo's Restaurant in nearby Pomona, which for me carries a particularly frightening memory because it was on one of these excursions where I almost got Peter killed. One of the unconventional lessons I learned from Peter was that you can't really do two things at once. He never bought into the heralded claims about "multitasking," and our near-miss only confirmed his conviction, which quickly also became mine.

I was driving east on our way to Rillo's, still engaged in conversation with Peter. So engaged that I did not see the car barreling down at us from the west. I turned left in front of the oncoming driver who had absolutely no time to react. Peter saw what was about to happen and yelled, which quickly got my attention. I stomped on the accelerator and made a rather reckless entry into the parking lot of the restaurant, missing the oncoming vehicle by a frighteningly small margin.

Peter never said a word as I sat there shaking and considering the "what ifs." Had he not screamed—had I not reacted—that driver would have crashed at a very high speed into the passenger side of my rental car, killing the smartest man on the planet, courtesy of me. I would likely only have been maimed, but Peter would have been quite dead.

Fortunately, he survived, as did our ongoing relationship. In those first annual meetings, it was strictly business, which was just fine with me. At that point, I was not necessarily thinking friendship but simply about success; a few sessions with Peter Drucker would surely help me uncover ways to grow my business by a few more percentage points. What I quickly learned is that Peter was not a technician and therefore quite uninterested in the practical metrics behind the creation of wealth. While I was certain he cared about the success of my business, I don't recall him ever asking to look at my balance sheet, nor did we spend much time doing the kind of strategic planning you might expect from a highly paid and even more highly regarded consultant. Instead, Peter elevated the narrative. He diverted my attention from the nuts and bolts of running a business and focused instead on the broader horizons of things such as character, vision, and responsibility.

> I was not necessarily thinking friendship but simply about success; a few sessions with Peter Drucker would surely help me uncover ways to grow my business by a few more percentage points.

THE QUESTIONS BEHIND THE QUESTION

In those early annual meetings, he would settle into his favorite wicker chair, pull out the letter I had sent him and page through it for a few seconds to refresh his memory, and then begin talking slowly in that heavy Austrian accent. He would begin with a question or topic that I had highlighted in my letter, but soon veer off into what seemed at the time was an entirely unrelated rabbit trail, and just as that was beginning to make sense he would step off that trail and onto another. And then another, and maybe one more before somehow he would circle back to my original question and by that time, it all made sense and I could see that despite the circuitous nature of his answer he always knew where he was going and, more importantly, why. His breadth of knowledge was stunning and influenced me to become a lifelong student of history and literature.

My friend Fred Smith once described Peter's way of answering a question: "He normally begins about a thousand years away from the point and goes in a very wide loop that arrives at the point exactly. He uses illustrations from many disciplines to shed light on the point he is making, and each story builds on the last. He wants you to think about your situation in a larger context."

Once, to a question I penned about leadership, Peter took me on a journey of all the great companies he had consulted with, dropping in occasional anecdotes about a CEO's leadership style or certain pitfalls that derailed another leader's effectiveness. Then he shifted into soliloquy about the uniqueness of television and its potential to change culture for better or for worse, and finally wrapped things up with this startling statement: "You know, Bob, you could be the CEO of NBC if you wanted to."

After an ever-so-brief rush of imagining myself at 30 Rockefeller Center, I realized that Peter wasn't actually encouraging me to update my resume. His "point"—which he had been making over the past forty-five minutes or so—was to instill in me the courage he knew I needed to successfully lead my family's business. He somehow saw the question behind my question, which probably had to do with a latent insecurity about being a big fish in a small pond. Did I really have what it takes to stay ahead of such a rapidly growing business?

That was Peter's way. When he started talking you weren't quite sure he understood the question, but by the time he finished you realized he had done more than just answer your question. He showed you the reason why you asked the question by getting at the core issue that had been hiding from you until he turned down the final backstretch and connected all the dots that had seemed so unrelated.

> When he started talking you weren't quite sure he understood the question, but by the time he finished you realized he had done more than just answer your question. He showed you the reason why you asked the question.

Then again, Peter could be very direct. In one of our regular meetings, Peter suggested I spend some time thinking about my personal goals—not just for my business but for my life. So the next time we met, I had my list of six goals for my life all set. I was determined to show the professor that I had taken his assignment seriously, and began to recite them: to make a certain amount of money . . . to stay married to my wife, Linda . . . to serve God by serving others . . . to grow culturally and intellectually . . . to engender high self-esteem for our son, Ross—and that was when Peter interrupted me rather abruptly.

"You can't make goals for other people!" he stated with authority. "You can only set goals for yourself, which might include how you want to treat Ross. But only he can determine his goals—not you or anyone else."

Of course, he was absolutely right, and probably protected me from the kind of frustration and angst that often comes when well-intentioned parents attempt to overlay their own goals onto their children. My own intentions, I like to think, were both noble and practical. Ross was our only son and would likely be my successor. As his father I naturally wanted the very best for him—what parent doesn't? And as the caretaker of the family business, I wanted it to remain in competent hands. Ross was a person of great promise, but as Peter took great care to point out, he had to be his own man.

GAINING THROUGH LOSS

As things turned out, Ross gave us little reason to doubt his ability to not only run the company, but take it to even greater levels of success than his father. After he graduated from Texas Christian University, he moved to Denver to take a job as an investment banker. In his first year, 1986, he made $150,000, and as he began his second year in the deal-making business he was on track to see his income soar by more than $500,000. Most important to me was the fact that he was a good human being, unaffected by his financial success and blessed with a heart for others. He loved life with all its pleasures and ambiguities, and Linda and I followed his transformation from child to man with thankful hearts. In ways that may seem odd to you but absolutely real to me, Ross was one of my great heroes.

So when on the evening of January 3, 1987, I received a call from my brother informing me that Ross and two of his friends had attempted to swim across the Rio Grande River in south Texas and were missing, I flew down to the spot where they had last been seen and tried to rescue my hero. I hired airplanes, helicopters, boats, trackers with dogs—everything that money could buy. But by three o'clock that afternoon, I looked into the eyes of one of the trackers and knew that I would never see Ross again in this life.

As I wrote of this event in my first book, *Halftime*, this was something I couldn't dream my way out of, plan my way out of, or buy my way out of. The only way I would get through this was to *trust* my way out of it—to accept and absorb whatever grace people might bring to me at this terrible time.

When it became clear that Ross was gone, I flew back home to Tyler to be with Linda, and one of the first of those people who offered the grace I so dearly needed was Peter. Somehow he had learned of our tragic loss and called me. The winter sun hovered just above the horizon, casting long shadows that seemed to echo the sadness that flooded my entire being as I settled into a chair to take his call. For the next several minutes we had a very affectionate, compassionate, intensely personal conversation and his sadness for my losing Ross almost seemed to match my own. And then he said something that was remarkable in its candor even as it echoed my own thoughts.

> His real business—his primary interest
> in management—is not for the sake
> of business itself, but for the people it
> touches, serves, and influences.

"Isn't it a shame that it takes this kind of moment for you and me to have the kind of conversation we just had?"

And yet, as I was only beginning to learn from Peter, his real business—his primary interest in management—was not for the sake of business itself, but for the people it touches, serves, and influences. For the first time in our relationship as client-consultant, I realized that Peter cared as much for me as a fellow human being as he did for me as a young, ambitious entrepreneur.

And I began to see him less as the highly-revered "father of management" and more as a fellow human being—albeit an unusual one.

5

EXTRAORDINARILY ORDINARY

"Books about business deal with functions and strategies—the mechanics of running a successful company. Fiction teaches you about human beings—how they think, how they behave, what's important to them. I'm more interested in people than I am in how businesses work."

—PETER DRUCKER

IN MANY WAYS, Peter was an anomaly. On the one hand, he was probably the most focused individual I've ever known. In the same way Shakespeare was utterly focused on writing his huge folio of plays and Mozart was utterly focused on his music, Peter saw himself primarily as a writer and exhibited incredible discipline to that calling. When he died at age 95 in 2005, he was still working on his next book. He never let the temptations of success or the demands on his time get in the way of his writing.

Other than his wife, Doris, and his children, his work was his greatest love. How else could you explain the thirty-nine books and countless articles and essays he wrote for some of the most prestigious periodicals in the world? He was incapable of being diverted. He didn't follow sports. He didn't watch television. He didn't play golf. He did not pursue titles or awards, equally unimpressed with both. But don't confuse his ardor for work with the common executive disease of workaholism. Unlike many of the captains of industry he counseled, Peter was not driven by an insatiable appetite for success (and all the perks that come with it). Just the royalties on his book sales would have given him the resources to own a bigger house and pursue all the diversions available to wealthy individuals, but he had all he needed: a house within walking distance to work and a job that allowed him to do what he loved. Peter's mental horizons were boundless. The examples he used came from every century and every continent.

THE GREAT MUSHROOM HUNT

Even Peter's "vacations" had a certain functionality about them. Every summer he and Doris, along with a gaggle of grandchildren and a large box of books, would head off to the Rocky Mountains where they rented a spare, rustic cabin in Estes Park. It was more for Doris than for him because Doris loved to hike in the mountains. Not so much Peter. So Doris would hike while Peter remained in the cabin reading. When he finished a book, he either threw it away or donated it to someone so they wouldn't have to cart the box of books back home.

That's not to say Peter was all work and no play. He loved to laugh, even if it was at his own expense—which was often the case thanks to Doris's mischievous sense of humor. On one of their summer sojourns to Estes Park, Peter for some reason had decided to study mushrooms. Of course for Peter, assiduously reading through a couple of college-level textbooks wasn't enough. To really study mushrooms meant traipsing about the countryside, collecting as many varieties of fungi as he could find, and taking them back to the cabin for further examination.

One day Doris decided to join the hunt. She drove into town and searched the shops for the perfect specimen: a rubber replica of an edible mushroom. She could hardly contain her glee as she drove back, parked the car next to the cabin, and then headed down a trail her husband often trekked on his daily hunt for mushrooms. She picked out a conspicuous spot alongside the path, scooped a small hole in the soil and "planted" her rubber mushroom.

Sure enough, the next day Peter rushed back from his jaunt into the woods, waving his prized trophy. Doris did her best to play along, but finally burst out laughing as Peter struggled to slice the rubber mushroom with a kitchen knife. When he realized he had been so artfully deceived, he laughed right along with Doris. He did the same every April 1st since the day they were married, even though the April Fool's trick never varied: Doris sewed the legs of his pajamas shut, and Peter always feigned surprise.

> More than anyone else I know, Peter lived the good life not so much because of the leisure and creature comforts he could have had, but because he was doing exactly what he loved to do.

More than anyone else I know, Peter lived the good life not so much because of the leisure and creature comforts he could have had, but because he was doing exactly what he loved to do. That alone is a lesson worthy of our emulation. Work that you enjoy and that makes a contribution to a greater good ought to be enough to make any of us happy.

Peter was an original thinker, a self-created, one-of-a-kind individual who comes along every two or three centuries. This may sound overly flattering, but in my opinion Peter was to management what Shakespeare was to literature. He was an indefatigable observer of human nature and the interaction of human beings with one another and with circumstances. To that end, Peter wrote from what he observed. His books were notorious among so-called management scholars for their absence of footnotes, betraying his disdain for much of the publishing that came out of academia. He once referred to one of the most prestigious academic journals in the United States as being "written by people who cannot write for an audience that does not read." He rarely spoke of it, but he was repeatedly snubbed by universities and business schools whose list of guest lecturers and adjunct faculty never seemed to include his name. I know it bothered him to be so ignored by the academic community, but he didn't get mad. He got even—by simply continuing on the positive track of his work for a lifetime and influencing at least two generations of CEOs and entrepreneurs across the public, private, and nonprofit sectors.

A TYPEWRITER AND SOME POSTAGE STAMPS

What I found most amazing about his prolific output was that he pretty much nailed it on his very first draft—and all without the use of a computer. He would pound out his manuscript on an old Brother typewriter and then hand it off to an editor who had precious little work to do to tidy it up for the printer. Once during lunch with him at Rillo's, he corrected a piece he had written earlier that day for *The Wall Street Journal*. One handwritten run-through over lunch before sending it off to New York.

In addition to his writing, he also worked with MBA students at Claremont, consulted with Fortune 500 companies, and accepted invitations from all over the world as a much-in-demand speaker. And yet, to my knowledge, he never had an office other than the tiny one in his home. I don't believe I ever heard him utter the word *telecommute*, but he was a pioneer of the "work from home" movement. When he needed copies made of an article he had written or an assignment for his students, he walked to a local Kinko's (now FedEx Office), grabbed the little cartridge-like thing, snapped it in place on a printer, printed his copies, then took the little cartridge thing to the counter so the clerk could charge him for his copies.

The thought of Peter Drucker doing his own copying and then reaching into his back pocket, pulling out his wallet, and then paying the guy for maybe fifteen copies was too much for me. So one day I offered to buy him a copy machine.

"I don't need one, Bob."

"What about a fax machine?"

"Don't need one of those either."

I offered to hire him an administrative assistant to handle all his clerical work, since I knew when Peter mailed an article to, say, *Harvard Business Review*, he carefully folded the pages, stuffed them into an envelope onto which he had carefully typed the address with his manual typewriter, and then licked the postage stamps before affixing them on the envelope. Every time I arrived at his house, the big mailbox next to the doorway was always stuffed with outgoing mail. I just felt it would be more efficient for him to have someone else do all that "gofer" work for him. He would have none of that.

> He appreciated technology, welcoming it as a tool to assist people to work more efficiently. But he wasn't about to let conventions of the day interrupt or interfere with the processes he had developed for his own work.

I would like to attribute this to his Old World frugality—and certainly there was a bit of that at play—but what I learned from observing Peter is that he possessed an uncanny self-knowledge and understood exactly what worked best for him. He appreciated technology, welcoming it as a tool to assist people to work more efficiently. But he wasn't about to let conventions of the day interrupt or interfere with the processes he had developed for his own work. And how could you argue with that, given his productivity? There are a lot of authors and leaders who will never match Peter's output, either in quantity or quality, despite their having the latest wireless devices and an army of assistants and researchers working for them.

You might be tempted to confuse Peter's focus and discipline with a sort of rigid parochialism or cultural myopia, but that would be a mistake. It was his focus and discipline—along with his insatiable curiosity—that allowed him to travel freely outside the lanes of his chosen field of expertise. Peter may have invented the modern discipline of management, but he was no management geek.

MANAGEMENT AS A HUMAN ACTIVITY

One of the first things I noticed on my early visits to his home were the books on his shelves: mostly fiction, with occasional histories—Shakespeare, Dickens, de Tocqueville—but a conspicuous absence of "business books." After about my third or fourth visit, my curiosity got the best of me.

"Peter, it appears as if you read a lot of novels," I said. "Somehow I would have thought your bookshelves would have been lined with books related more to your discipline."

He paused for a second, a whimsical smile momentarily forming before he answered with typical authority. Peter spoke as he wrote, with razor-sharp clarity marked by an economy of words. "Books about business deal with functions and strategies—the mechanics of running a successful company," he said. "Fiction teaches you about human beings—how they think, how they behave, what's important to them. I'm more interested in people than I am in how businesses work."

I came to learn that this was quintessential Drucker, a man who always described management as a "human activity" rather than a tool or process for running a business. He was fond of explaining that the only way you're going to have a functioning society and, therefore, not a fascist society like he came from in Europe, is if all the units of society do what they're intended to do. It is management that enables these organizations to work properly. It makes symphonies work, armies work, schools work, television stations work. Peter devoted his life to giving a language and structure to the discipline of management, where there wasn't any before.

This is what separated Peter from so many business "experts." Through my good friend Joseph Maciariello, who collaborated with Peter and knew him as well as anyone, I learned that Peter had attended a series of seminars in the 1930s led by economist John Maynard Keynes. When I asked Peter his thoughts about Keynes he responded with characteristic succinctness: "Keynes was interested in the behavior of commodities, particularly money, while I have always been interested in the behavior of human beings. I discovered listening to Keynes that I wasn't interested in money. It was a major turning point in my life."

Sometimes that interest in the behavior of people yielded humorous results. Once, while traveling in Japan, Peter decided to sample a bit of the local culture by attending a special tea ceremony whose origins date back several hundred years. It was conducted in Kyoto by the Master of Tea, a Mr. Sen. The ceremony took place in a room of perfect yet simple beauty, with smooth stones gracing the *tatami* floor and a small lacquered table inlaid with mother of pearl behind which Mr. Sen knelt in his ornate *kimono*. Peter knelt opposite Mr. Sen and for the next forty-five minutes watched in fascination the quiet, almost mystical ritual. Finally, Mr. Sen poured the tea he had carefully brewed in a three-hundred-year-old vessel, and Peter dutifully sipped it in silence.

After he set his ceramic cup onto the table, Mr. Sen bowed and asked Peter if he would like another cup. What Peter didn't know was that the question was part of the ritual and the appropriate answer was always a polite no. Peter so enjoyed the tea and thought the second cup would allow him to engage Mr. Sen in some conversation that he gregariously said yes to the offer of another cup, only to have the Grand Master of Tea now feel compelled to perform the forty-five-minute ritual all over again.

Every time he shared that story with me, he had a great

laugh at his own expense. But that was Peter—curious about people, what made them tick, why they did what they did. He sometimes described himself as a "social ecologist." Others often described Peter as the "greatest futurist alive," but he had little regard for crystal-ball predictions. The way he put it was, "You can't predict the future. What you *can* do is look out the window and see the futurity of present events."

Others often described Peter as the "greatest futurist alive," but he had little regard for crystal-ball predictions. The way he put it was, "You can't predict the future. What you can do is look out the window and see the futurity of present events."

With this insight, Peter was able to see things that most people could not see. Where others in his field tried to read the tea leaves of market research, Peter studied the broader cycles of history, demographics and, above all, people. It was by observing people and how they behaved that Peter accurately predicted the transition in America from an industrial economy to one powered by knowledge—probably the most extreme societal change in recorded history. From that same observation post he was one of the first to foresee the emergence of the information economy as well as the rise of new "superpowers" such as China, India, and South America.

As Steve Forbes wrote in *The Wall Street Journal*, "Peter Drucker's ability to prophesy—almost always correctly—was uncanny." If I thought I had learned a great deal from Peter through his books, our annual meetings became a sort of post-doctorate for me.

Peter had "eyes to see and ears to hear" and an unparalleled memory to recall and relate centuries of human interactions. It was impossible to spend time with Peter without learning something so obviously true that you wondered why you hadn't thought of it yourself.

6

LESSONS FROM PETER

"Peter began to have grave doubts about business and even capitalism itself. He no longer saw the corporation as an ideal space to create community. In fact, he saw nearly the opposite: a place where self-interest had triumphed over the egalitarian principles he long championed."

—JOHN BYRNE

I HAVE NEVER tried drugs or even mastered enough of the glossary of the drug culture to talk about it with any clarity or authority. However, I do know that the term "mainlining" refers to the practice of injecting a particular drug of choice directly into one's vein in order to get the fullest effect. It is an apt description of the practice by which I have been influenced most, mainlining from three sources: my wife, the Bible, and Peter Drucker.

I rely on Linda for a lot of things, but mostly her profound gift of empathy. My wealth could easily distance me from the ordinary challenges, hopes, and dreams of the majority of Americans. Linda keeps me grounded. I just follow her lead and pay attention to what she tells me. She helps me understand people who are unlike me, and in the process of doing that she protects me from making a fool of myself. For example, I let nothing get out in print under my name that she has not read and approved, even though it sometimes temporarily wounds my pride. Once I was so proud of something I wrote because I had used the phrase *de riguer* only to have her call my bluff by asking if I even knew what it meant before reminding me that no one else would either.

Mainlining Scripture for most of my adult life has, I hope, given me a reliable moral compass as well as a sense of my role in the story of God's journey with mankind. It also is what gives me the hope I need to live rather than exist. Or as the Danish philosopher Søren Kierkegaard put it: "The only way to avoid despair is to have faith that, in God's time, time and eternity become one. That both life and death are meaningful."

That leaves Peter, who I had begun mainlining before I ever met him, reading every word that he had written and resonating with it so much that it became part of my DNA. And through an in-person relationship that grew in depth and breadth each year for more than twenty years, I have long since ceased trying to determine what thoughts are mine and which come from Peter. I think it would be fair and accurate to say that most of the really good ideas I may have had over the years can trace their genesis back to Peter.

I have long since ceased trying to determine what thoughts are mine and which come from Peter. I think it would be fair and accurate to say that most of the really good ideas I may have had over the years can trace their genesis back to Peter.

For example, early into my run as CEO of our family business, I put a lot of emphasis on creating teams to address various challenges we faced. Even though I was the top dog and could pretty much run the company like a benevolent monarch, I relied heavily on the talent surrounding me. I think I may have inherently known that I simply was not smart enough to figure everything out on my own. But by that time I had been immersed in Peter's writing and probably recalled something that Peter wrote: "All work is for a team. No individual has the temperament and the skill to do every job. The purpose of a team is to make strengths productive and weaknesses irrelevant." To this day, I never approach a new challenge without first assembling a team.

Earlier I shared the one time Peter's advice sent me chasing a major business deal that eventually caused me to lose a million dollars. I guess I was trying to demonstrate that Peter was human and that despite the loss, I never lost confidence in his counsel. In fairness, it was a major lesson from Peter that kept this from being an even bigger disaster.

WE'RE NOT IN KANSAS ANYMORE

My company, Buford Television Inc., found a way to become profitable serving small- to midsize cities like my home town of Tyler, Texas; Ft. Smith, Arkansas; and Sioux Falls, South Dakota. We accomplished our success with a combination of old-fashioned customer service and what at the time was innovative use of technology. For example, all the people who worked for us went to small colleges and lived in small towns, and that helped them understand the customers we served. In the bigger cities, the people who had responsibility for local cable companies were elected officials. In these tiny small towns where we operated, it was your next-door neighbor. If your next-door neighbor can't get a signal on Super Bowl Sunday, that is not an abstract problem. Early on we learned the value of not just serving your customer, but knowing him and understanding his unique needs (another Drucker axiom).

We were also among the first to set up a call center that

dispatched our installation and repair people in an efficient fashion. These technicians worked out of their homes and got their work orders sent to their computers. The computer was tied to a satellite uplink that gave them directions to their next assignment, which reduced their drive time. When a customer was wired for cable, someone's cable was fixed, or some other task was accomplished, the technician would go back out to his truck, punch the information into his computer, and in a nanosecond it was on the customer's billing record. This is standard operating procedure today, but twenty years ago this was cutting edge and helped drive our profitability.

Although we were doing quite well—and growing fast—I was smart enough to know that growth doesn't just happen, and so I was always looking for ways to improve the performance of the family business. At the time, I had an attorney in Washington who also represented ABC, and he thought I should get into subscription television—a single-channel, over-the-air sports and movie service aimed at larger markets such as New York, Chicago, and Los Angeles, which in those days were not wired. At my next annual meeting with Peter, I ran the idea by him, and he thought it made sense. When a big-city lawyer and Peter Drucker pick what they think will be a winner, you tend to pay attention. So when the opportunity came to get into subscription television, I jumped in with more enthusiasm than experience—and almost immediately realized it was a bad decision.

Now, instead of working with municipalities to get my cables into their well-manicured neighborhoods, I was negotiating to rent expensive antennas on tops of skyscrapers like the Hancock Building in Chicago. Instead of running cables throughout familiar territory in Texas, I was launched into an entirely new orbit as I calculated the metrics of purchasing satellite uplinks. When I walked into the Willow Brook Country Club in Tyler, everyone knew me. When I got off the plane at O'Hare airport in Chicago, I was just another suit and briefcase. With a checkbook. Subscription television, as I was learning, was not cheap. I now had a rapidly expanding payroll to meet and a shopping list of pricey equipment to buy. To paraphrase Dorothy in "The Wizard of Oz," I was not in Tyler anymore.

My story might have ended here had it not been for a concept I learned from Peter: planned abandonment. If you are diagnosed with cancer, don't spend a lot of time thinking about your options. Get rid of it as quickly as you can. It was not unusual for Peter to begin a meeting by saying, "Tell me what you're *not* doing." In other words, not everything you try is going to work out, so what have you decided not to do? What have you quit doing so that you can focus more on those things that will produce results? When I shared with Peter the debacle of my venture into subscription television, his verdict confirmed what I already knew I had to do. I found a buyer and lost $1 million overall on the deal, one of the best business decisions I've ever made. Three years after purchasing my company, the new owner's annual report showed a loss of $72 million.

> It was not unusual for Peter to begin a meeting by saying, "Tell me what you're not doing." In other words, not everything you try is going to work out, so what have you decided not to do?

PERFORMANCE, NOT POTENTIAL

One time I decided to take one of my company's top executives with me to one of my mentoring meetings with Peter. He was relatively new and I wanted to give him exposure to Peter's wisdom and teaching. Peter, as always, was gracious and made him feel right at home as we began working through the long letter I had sent him earlier. We had a delightful day together and I could see that my colleague thoroughly enjoyed the experience of learning from one of the great minds in the world.

A few days later I spoke with Peter on the phone about something, and after our brief conversation, I gave in to my curiosity and asked Peter if he thought this particular executive was a good man.

"Good for what?" he replied in his typically direct manner and then went on to explain a concept that I have applied henceforth in personnel matters.

"With people, you focus on performance, not potential. You focus on what they can do—their strengths—not on what they might do sometime in the future. What they can't do is someone else's job."

Peter frequently used the metaphor of a symphony conductor when he talked about management. A conductor would never ask an oboe player to play the violin, or vice versa. The role of the conductor is to make sure the right people are playing the right instruments so that when the baton came down, the symphony made great music.

Every venture I have undertaken, whether profit or non-profit, has been a play for rapid growth requiring almost continuous innovation and entrepreneurial energy. More than once I have employed a person who performed well in a maintenance role in a large, prestigious organization. It never seems to work out. It is the difference between Special Forces and holding down a Pentagon job.

Peter taught me to never try turning an oboe player into a violinist. I learned from him not to complain about people's weaknesses but to always focus on their strengths and move them into areas where those strengths can thrive.

HOW ORGANIZATIONS DIE

One of the most important lessons I learned from Peter inevitably, in my view, turned our client-consultant relationship into more of a partnership. That lesson was his conviction that an organization begins to die the day it begins to be run for the benefit of the insiders and not for the benefit of the customers. It was around this time in the mid- to late-1980s that I sensed a shift in his thinking about the corporate America he had spent so much time advising. He began to question whether or not corporations were helping to create the kind of well-ordered and fully functioning society he envisioned.

> One of the most important lessons I learned from Peter . . . was his conviction that an organization begins to die the day it begins to be run for the benefit of the insiders and not for the benefit of the customers.

Writing in *BusinessWeek*, John Byrne observed that around this period of economic prosperity in America, Peter "began to have grave doubts about business and even capitalism itself.

He no longer saw the corporation as an ideal space to create community. In fact, he saw nearly the opposite: a place where self-interest had triumphed over the egalitarian principles he long championed."

Peter had disdain for the way large corporations piled up huge profits, not so much because he was opposed to profit but because those same corporations fired thousands of workers as they lavished huge compensation packages on their executives. "A business that does not show a profit at least equal to its cost of capital is socially irresponsible," he wrote in *Managing in a Time of Great Change*. But he also believed "the worship of high profit margin is likely to damage—if not destroy—the business" (*Five Deadly Business Sins* online program). He argued—to no avail—that corporations should compensate their CEOs no more than twenty times what the rank and file made. Peter saw the raising of capital as a way for the corporation to better accomplish its mission, which was to better provide value for its customers, rather than to provide value for the five guys in the executive suite.

And it wasn't just the corporation that felt the sting of his criticism. Peter increasingly viewed government as being run for the benefit of the insiders rather than its citizen customers. "Fifty or sixty years ago, government programs delivered," he once wrote in an informal summary of his thoughts on the social sector. "They don't deliver anymore, not only in this country, but no place in the world. It's all good intentions, for which we pay taxes. The greatest achievement in the last, well, since World War II, is the social sector. It is the one thing in our country, and in the world, to stress. I'm very optimistic about the prospects for the social sector."

The numbing gridlock we see in our legislature today is a perfect example of Peter's analysis that such ineffectiveness is always the result of an organization looking out for itself rather than those it was intended to serve.

It would be easy, then, to dismiss Peter's disenchantment with business and government as just another cranky septuagenarian who has nothing better to do than grouse about the way things are. Except Peter was never about the way things are. He always maintained a vision for the way things could be. Plus, he still had a lot in his tank—retirement was never an option for him—so if business and government weren't getting the job done, he'd find something else.

And thanks to Peter, retirement was forever banished from my own vocabulary.

7

SUCCESS TO SIGNIFICANCE

"My performance as president and CEO was becoming more important than my performance as a human being."

—BOB BUFORD

AROUND THE TIME Peter was becoming increasingly disillusioned with corporate America, I began to hear a still, small voice whispering a haunting question into the deepest chambers of my soul: "What are you going to do with all that you've been given?"

I had been given a lot.

My business was still growing at a phenomenal rate greater than 25 percent annually. Even though I always followed Peter's recommendation that my compensation remain below twenty times the average of my employees, I had exceeded my goals for accumulation of net worth. During the week Linda and I lived in a wonderfully appointed penthouse in Dallas and then retreated to our 250-acre "gentleman's farm" in Tyler.

I drove a Cadillac, Linda a Jaguar. We could—and did—travel anywhere in the world we wanted.

My marriage was secure and eminently rewarding. I had somehow escaped the usual addictions that sneak into the lives of many successful businessmen. I gave generously to many good causes. I even taught Sunday school at my church. I was in the prime of my life with a clear and attractive road ahead of me: groom my successor and eventually cash out and live the good life.

But the whispering continued: Is my work still the center of my life? What is my truest purpose? My destiny? What does it really mean to have it all? What would my life look like if it really turned out well?

> But the whispering continued: Is my work still the center of my life? What is my truest purpose? My destiny? What does it really mean to have it all?

"YOU FRIGHTEN ME"

And then, in one of those unscripted events that seemed to come out of nowhere, I was given a little nudge—well, more of a slap—that infused those questions with a greater sense of urgency.

I was on a mission, and I pursued it with such intensity that my administrative assistant—a woman about fifteen years older than I—confronted me with some unsolicited and initially unwelcome criticism. I was flying all over the country chasing deals and doing whatever it took to add to the bottom line of my company, but this brave lady saw something that bothered her.

"Mr. Buford, I think you need to know that you frighten me," she carefully began, obviously aware that this was not the best way to begin a conversation with your boss. "You are so concerned about outperforming everyone else and making a lot of money that I'm afraid you're going to lose things that are valuable to you."

This is what we sometimes refer to in the business world as a CLM: "career limiting move." And I will admit that at first her words stung. But I had already learned from Peter two things that I had the presence of mind to apply to this humbling encounter. First, Peter felt that a leader needed to pay attention to those he or she was trying to lead. And second, Peter approached problems by asking questions. So I paid attention to my assistant's criticism and then asked myself two questions: Was she right? And, if so, what did I need to do about it?

That first question was pretty easy to answer, though it is amazing how susceptible we are to self-delusion. As it turned out, my assistant knew me better than I knew myself, and her courage rather inelegantly removed the scales from my eyes. My performance as president and CEO was becoming more important than my performance as a human being.

LIFE WAS GOOD . . . SORT OF

Determining what I needed to do to correct that was not as easy. This was not a midlife crisis, nor was this soul-searching interruption brought on by anything pathological. I wasn't addicted to anything, legal or illegal. I was fortunate to be working with people I respected and admired. Ten years earlier I had written down a list of life goals, and I was well on my way to accomplishing all of them. Quite frankly, I rather liked my life.

But I could not shake the feeling that despite all the success I was having in both my professional and personal lives, I might be missing something even better.

That something is what I eventually described as significance—investing yourself in a mission or dream that transcends material success and aligns with your most deeply held core values. Because of my strong faith and commitment to the church, I initially thought that significance would involve some form of church work—most likely preceded by a few years in seminary—and quite honestly that frightened me. Ministry—as I understood it—was the antithesis to the real world in which I had performed for the past twenty-five years. I quickly abandoned the notion of enrolling in seminary or circulating my resume to faith-based nonprofits, but I couldn't ignore the hauntingly persistent voice inviting me to make some fairly radical changes in my life.

> I could not shake the feeling that despite all the success I was having in both my professional and personal lives, I might be missing something even better.

Whenever I faced new challenges or opportunities in my business, I began by drawing up a strategic plan that not only provided a road map for moving forward, but a yardstick for measuring my effectiveness. I decided I needed a strategic plan for *me*! I hired a brilliant and demanding strategic planning coach to help me with the process. Though he was not a man of religious faith, after spending some time with me and asking me a lot of questions, he identified two things that were extremely important to me: money and God. And then he told me that he could not help me develop a plan for my life until I chose one over the other. He did not care which I chose but assured me I would not find the direction I was looking for until I chose either God or money as being the primary recipient of my loyalty. Once I made the choice, he could help me make the transition from the success I had enjoyed to the significance I coveted.

I describe this process in greater detail in my first book, *Halftime*, but I will spare you the suspense: I chose God. Once I had made that commitment, we developed a plan that called for me to devote about 20 percent of my time to my business with the remaining 80 percent of my time given over to God. But what exactly did that mean? What would sharing my time, talent, and treasure with God look like? There were hundreds—if not thousands—of Christian ministries and organizations that might welcome a successful Christian businessman who had decided to spend most of his time and money in service to God. But as I had learned from Peter, to get the most effective results you must "build on the islands of health and strength." In other words, if I really wanted to do something of significance—something that would prosper and grow and make a difference in the world long after I'm gone—I would need to invest where there was the greatest chance of rapid growth and a high return.

This is totally counterintuitive to most philanthropy. Conventional wisdom suggests that I find the most desperate inner-city mission in town, swoop in with a handful of money, and rescue it, but Peter turned that notion on its head. In addition to his belief that thinking small yielded small results, I suspect he shared my own view that although it is tempting, playing the rescuer is a bit egocentric.

I had grown my business by acquiring healthy broadcast television stations and cable companies that offered tremendous potential, so it made sense to me that this would be how I would approach significance. Peter also warned against wasting my time tilting against the establishment. "Look for people who are receptive to what you want to do, rather than push rocks uphill the rest of your life," he cautioned.

He also told me not to focus on dribs and drabs, or "fritter my energy away," as he actually said it. That's what most philanthropists do—a little donation here, and a little donation there, and they wake up at the end of the year and have nothing to show for it except that they went to a lot of charity balls. I purposely leave town on Thursday. Charity balls in Dallas all occur between Thursday and Saturday night, providing regular opportunities to do just as Peter had warned against.

GIVING IS NOT A RESULT

As I was casting about looking for ways to invest myself more fully into faith-based activities, I accepted an invitation to be on the advisory board of a ministry that was affiliated with a seminary. I went to one meeting where I presented a proposal over which I had thought long and hard and included funding that I would help provide. It wasn't accepted but referred to a committee for further study, and I realized that it would probably take another several years to push this thing through the bureaucracy of a seminary. When I shared that experience with Peter he said, "You need to use your energy where you can get results." He wisely steered me away from seminaries because, in his words, "I don't think they really want to know what they need."

Peter encouraged me to look for things that make a quantum difference, not incremental gains. "Giving is not a result," he frequently reminded me. "Changed lives are!"

Peter encouraged me to look for things that make a quantum difference, not incremental gains. "Giving is not a result," he frequently reminded me. "Changed lives are!"

Finally, Peter encouraged me to "look for things that are ready to happen." Timing is everything. My efforts would be multiplied if they converged with opportunities that were already looking to expand. Yet he added to this advice something that not only demonstrated how much he had learned by observing me, but also underscored his optimism that I would indeed find what I was looking for:

> *You have two fundamental commitments. One is a religious one in the sense that you believe in another world, and the other is an existential one, related to human existence. You believe that what matters is not how bright you are, how much money you have, how many degrees you have, but that you are one of God's children. We'll find a place for you; you will find a place for yourself.*

All great advice, but where was that place—that healthy opportunity—in the faith community? What new, transformative phenomenon was an ember or spark that needed help in fanning it into a wildfire?

I turned to my good friend Fred Smith, who introduced me to two gentlemen who sat at the helm of a remarkable and successful Christian magazine company based in the western suburbs of Chicago. Christianity Today Inc. grew out of its flagship eponymous magazine, *Christianity Today*, which was founded by the renowned evangelist Dr. Billy Graham. When Harold Myra and Paul Robbins were named CEO and CFO, respectively, the magazine was struggling like most religious periodicals, heavily subsidized to make up the difference between increasing costs and anemic revenue from advertising and subscriptions.

They not only quickly put Christianity Today's financial house in order, but added six other specialty magazines, all pulling their own weight and contributing to a healthy bottom line. In the process, Harold and "Robbie" developed an uncanny ability to identify the legitimate leaders and innovators in the robust movement that has come to be known as evangelicalism. Who better than these two to help me find just the right niche for me to engage my time, talent, and investment capital into something that would have a lasting impact on the world?

I arranged to meet them at the modest headquarters of their business in Carol Stream, Illinois, and shared with them my desire to spend the rest of my life—and most of my money—on a faith-based enterprise that had the potential to make a huge difference in the world. I made it clear that I wasn't looking to make a major donation to some organization in hopes of getting my name on a building. I explained that not only would this venture become the primary focus of my philanthropy, but

I intended to devote as much energy, time, and expertise to it as I had to my own company.

If they thought I was crazy, they masked their suspicions masterfully. After politely listening to my request for assistance in turning the world upside down, they told me about a small but growing group of pastors and ministry leaders who were unlike any traditional understanding of what a pastor was. They explained that these were entrepreneurial leaders who had built very large, dynamic churches largely through innovation and a laser-like focus on engaging contemporary culture. Most of these pastors started their churches from scratch, inviting people from their neighborhoods into their homes to study the Bible and eventually building attractive "campuses" that drew thousands each weekend to services characterized by contemporary music and practical, inspiring "teaching." A few of these pastors had been successful businessmen, using their gifts of leadership and management to develop incredibly effective churches. Others had taken their traditional churches and transformed them into highly effective and holistic ministry centers. The common denominator of these pastors was their ability to reach people who had pretty much given up on "religion" and had no interest in church.

Harold and Robbie expressed some concern that these somewhat renegade pastors were isolated, often facing criticism from their respective denominations or other churches. Perhaps they would benefit from someone like me who could bring them together, let them share best practices with each other, and generally encourage them.

I loved the idea. I had never really connected the word "entrepreneur" with pastor, but the more I thought about it, the more it made sense. If God's idea of the church was conceived as a strategy for transforming the world, why not go about it in the most professional and effective manner possible? And if all knowledge comes from God—which I believe it does—why not use the "knowledge" of strategic planning, management principles, consumer research, communications, and the like to introduce more people to what we sometimes glibly call the Good News?

> I had never really connected the word "entrepreneur" with pastor, but the more I thought about it, the more it made sense. If God's idea of the church was conceived as a strategy for transforming the world, why not go about it in the most professional and effective manner possible?

As I flew back to Dallas I was convinced of two things. One, I had found my new calling. Two, I had no idea what to do about it. I can say with almost absolute certainty that I was as unknown to those pastors as they were to me. And although I have attended church most of my life, my church was fairly small and comfortably traditional. What could I possibly offer these pastors that would make them want to get on a plane and fly somewhere for another meeting?

8

SECOND HALF
CONSPIRACY

*"Your mission, Bob, is to transform
the latent energy of American
Christianity into active energy."*

—PETER DRUCKER

YOU CANNOT GROW up in Texas and not be a football fan. Notwithstanding my own brief career as a middling left end for my high-school football team, I fully embraced the official religion of the Lone Star state, following both my alma mater, the University of Texas Longhorns, and who else but America's team—the Dallas Cowboys. So when I began experiencing unsettling thoughts about my career and ambitions, it is not surprising that I looked to football for a metaphor to help me understand what was happening.

By the time I hit my early forties, I had devoted nearly twenty years to growing the family business. Peter and I had been meeting regularly for roughly seven or eight years, and our conversation gradually migrated from business—specifically

Buford Television Inc.—to what had always been his primary interest in "management": creating the conditions for a fully functioning society.

One of the demographic changes that Peter had observed was the increasing lifespan of the American worker, along with the shift from laborer to "knowledge worker." Up until the mid-Twentieth Century, life expectancy in the United States peaked at around fifty-five years. By the end of the Twentieth Century, that threshold had risen to seventy-four years. Moreover, instead of milking cows twice a day or performing the same monotonous task on an assembly line, all those GI-bill college-educated men began working at less physically demanding jobs as sales-men, engineers, managers, and the like.

HALFTIME

So when Peter told me that I had a full second career I could look forward to, I borrowed language from football to describe the disequilibrium I was feeling about my career. My "first half" had been devoted entirely to building our business. Like most men between the ages of twenty-five and forty, I was the true hunter-gatherer, chasing down the saber-toothed tiger of success. And although I had performed well beyond my own high expectations, I could not shake a nagging suspicion that the intensity with which I approached my work might cost me in other areas of my life. A question tugged at a distant corner of my mind: *What might you lose with all of this gaining?* I approached the end of the first half of my career knowing that I needed to change my game plan for the second half.

I was in halftime.

I knew my second half would focus more on aligning my time, treasure, and talent with my faith, and thanks to Paul and Robbie, I had narrowed my focus to a group of young "pastor entrepreneurs" who had developed very large churches. But beyond that, I was sort of clueless.

> Peter clearly understood and supported my vision for a second half that focused on my faith. Call it coincidence, or providence, but this new direction in my life occurred just as Peter was shifting his emphasis from the private sector to the nonprofit sector.

As all of this was going on, I maintained my regular meetings with Peter and, of course, shared with him my desire to transition into a more meaningful and significant "second half." Peter clearly understood and supported my vision for a second half that focused on my faith. Call it coincidence, or providence, but this new direction in my life occurred just as Peter was shifting his emphasis from the private sector to the nonprofit sector.

Still, there were uncertainties. Would the principles he espoused for managers and leaders translate into a community of organizations that depended so much on unpaid volunteers and whose revenue was largely determined by the generosity of ordinary citizens rather than the usual "value equation" found in the commercial world? As Peter would soon discover, the nonprofit sector presented a unique challenge as well as an opportunity to literally change the world. How could a man who cared deeply about the human condition resist?

He believed that the predominant need in our culture was for individuals to make their lives useful to themselves and others, and he believed nonprofit organizations were best suited to do that. According to Peter, nonprofit organizations were most effective in establishing "the functioning community and functioning democracy of tomorrow."

Serendipitously, given my own decision to focus more on my faith, Peter had been doing a lot of *pro bono* consulting with the Salvation Army. Where the public generally views this organization as people who ring a bell next to a red kettle during the holidays—or in previous generations, the uniformed half-dozen or so musicians playing their instruments on street corners—Peter studied them from the inside out and had high regard for them: "The Salvation Army is by far the most effective organization in the U.S.," he said in a 1997 interview in *Forbes*. "No one even comes close to it in respect to clarity of mission, ability to innovate, measurable results, dedication to putting money to maximum use."

His praise of the organization became the title of a book about it by Robert A. Watson and James Benjamin Brown: *The Most Effective Organization in the United States: Leadership Secrets of the Salvation Army*. But more than an endorsement for a book, they reflected Peter's many years of studying the organization and reflected his assessment of their effectiveness in meeting human need. As he told me once, "I look forward to meeting the people of the Salvation Army because whenever I sit down with them, I just find myself transported; their spirit is so wonderful, the joy of those people."

He knew the clientele served by the Salvation Army: "the poorest of the poor and the meanest of the mean"; he resonated with its mission of transforming down-and-outers. But more important, he knew how well the organization *performed*. Recovery rates for those who entered the Salvation Army's alcohol rehabilitation centers hovered around 45 percent, compared with 25 percent for most other treatment programs.

In its misdemeanor recovery program in which parole services are provided for first-time offenders, the success rate is about 80 percent.

According to James Osborne, a forty-year veteran of the Salvation Army and Southern U.S. Territorial Commander in Atlanta, Georgia, Peter's influence on the Salvation Army was "mammoth and beneficial." Two examples come to mind. One of the first things Peter did when he consulted with an organization was to ask them about their mission—what it was they intend to do. In a *Harvard Business Review* article he wrote, "The best nonprofits devote a great deal of time to defining their organization's mission. They avoid sweeping statements full of good intentions and focus, instead, on objectives that have clear-cut implications for the work their members perform—staff and volunteers both." Peter succintly paraphrased the Salvation Army's mission statement as: "Take the losers, the rejects of society and make self-respecting citizens out of them."

Peter also believed that the non-profit sector should assess the performance of their employees just as systematically and rigorously as the private sector. Rather than hold on to under-performing employees, as is often done with nonprofits, he recommended a frank assessment of the employee's deficiencies and additional training to address those deficiencies. In other words, a second chance, but with the same expectations in place. Through Peter's influence, the Salvation Army has a formal system in place to evaluate the performance of all its employees. Remarkably, of those employees whose performance is deficient and who are given a second chance, approximately 60 percent are successfully retrained and returned to productive service.

> Peter also believed that the non-profit sector should assess the performance of their employees just as systematically and rigorously as the private sector.

But most significantly, Peter treated the Salvation Army with the same respect and professionalism he offered his more high-profile clients such as General Motors. The fact that he was not paid or that they were not a multibillion-dollar corporation made no difference in the way he approached his assignment with them, which was to help them do what they did more efficiently and with greater results.

To honor his years of generous service to them, on November 6, 2001, the Salvation Army gave him one of their highest awards: the Evangeline Booth Award. The award is reserved for those who have provided long and distinguished service to the organization and who reflect "the spirit, commitment, and innovative vision of Evangeline, daughter of Salvation Army's founders, William and Catherine Booth."

Peter saw the Salvation Army as fully functioning, contributing, and transformational. To him, these were the defining characteristics of any of any successful organization but increasingly felt that the social sector could do it best.

TRANSFORMING AMERICA'S LATENT ENERGY

As I began to share with Peter my interest in doing something for a group of pastors, he listened carefully as I tried to explain the types of churches they led and how they were attracting large numbers of people who had previously not been inclined to have much to do with church. As far as I know, he knew virtually nothing about this new movement within American Christianity. But as I had seen so many times previously, Peter was a quick learner. In fact, it was Peter who distilled my somewhat disparate thinking into a mission statement that has guided me into a "second half" of significance. It was one of those moments that you never forget.

Peter had enthusiastically agreed to be interviewed before a good-sized audience of evangelical entrepreneurs at a conference hosted by the organization Fred Smith and I by now had formed called Leadership Network. The meeting was to be held at the Biltmore Hotel in Los Angeles. I hired a car to drive the two of us from Claremont to the hotel, leaving early enough to make sure we got there on time. As it turned out, we arrived well in advance of Peter's interview, so we went to the suite we had rented for him, and after I finished yet another iteration of what I wanted to do with the rest of my life, he sat silent for a moment and then spoke in a voice that to my ears sounded like the voice of God himself:

"Your mission, Bob, is to transform the latent energy of American Christianity into active energy."

Just like that, he nailed it. He took my meandering thoughts that had been fermenting for the past few years and articulated exactly what I wanted to do. According to most pollsters, anywhere from 70 to 85 percent of Americans consider themselves Christians. And on any given Sunday, roughly 45 percent of all Americans go to church. You would think that with so many Christians among us, we would have safer neighborhoods, less crime, fewer children going to school hungry, healthier marriages, and other distinguishing features of a "fully functioning society," to borrow from Peter. Unfortunately, despite all this religious activity, we don't.

What would happen if all these Christians took their faith

seriously, living out the teachings of Jesus at work, at home, in their cities? What if they moved from being latent to becoming active—from going to church on Sundays to *being* the church every day?

CONNECTING THE INNOVATORS

I knew I needed some type of structure or vehicle from which to operate, so with Fred Smith's help, I launched Leadership Network, whose mission at the time was to "identify, connect, and help high-capacity Christian leaders multiply their impact." Our initial idea was to be sort of a fly on the wall, listening to church leaders—primarily senior pastors of churches with more than a thousand in attendance. We hoped to foster a continuous stream of innovation by finding and connecting the innovators. We wanted them to share their ideas and teach others in their sphere of influence. We would use their credibility, not ours—we were the platform, not the show. Or as Peter once told me, "The fruit of your work grows on other people's trees."

The role of Leadership Network would be to provide connections, tools, and resources to help leaders minister more effectively. Our first major initiative was to try to arrange a series of meetings where Peter would share his wisdom with small groups of these pastors and church leaders. To be honest,

I wasn't sure any preacher in America knew who Peter was or, if they did, would view him as a reliable guide for their work in Christian ministry. Nor was I convinced that Peter would have any interest in spending time with a bunch of preachers.

I wasn't sure any preacher in America knew who Peter was or, if they did, would view him as a reliable guide for their work in Christian ministry. Nor was I convinced that Peter would have any interest in spending time with a bunch of preachers.

When I finally broached the subject with Peter, he basically said something like, "Well, yes—we *have* to do this." We didn't really have an agenda other than Peter knew that I wanted to see if his wisdom, which had so enriched my life, could be adapted to churches. Beyond that, our marching orders at Leadership Network were to identify the church leaders who would be most receptive to learning from a "secular" resource and invite them to come listen to Peter. As it turned out, I didn't exactly have to "sell" Peter. These people not only knew who Peter was but had read many of his books and held him in high esteem. All I had to do was mention his name, and the RSVPs began pouring in.

One of the first pastors to respond was a guy named Randy Pope, who had started Perimeter Church, a very successful and dynamic church in Atlanta. "When I got the invitation that mentioned Peter Drucker would be our guest, I could hardly believe it," Randy recently recalled for me. "I certainly knew Peter by his reputation and held him in the highest regard, and couldn't wait to hear what he had to say to a group of pastors."

To be honest, I was just as eager myself.

PETER AND THE PREACHERS

*"The function of management in a church
is to make the church more church-like,
not to make it more business-like."*

—PETER DRUCKER

THE PROMOTIONAL BROCHURE for the Estes Park
Center at the YMCA of the Rockies promises a venue "Where
Nature Inspires." Tucked away in a breathtaking stretch
of mountain range between the city of Estes Park and the
entrance to Rocky Mountain National Park, it's a popular des-
tination for individuals and groups looking for an escape from
the ordinary routines of life. Corporations, nonprofit organizations, and government groups send their people there for team
building and inspiration. It doesn't hurt that it's a good two
hours from Denver International Airport. Once you get there,
whatever was on your mind quickly fades.

The perfect place for a group of preachers who have a lot
on their minds.

It would be unfair to characterize every large-church pastor as hyperactive, but you don't take a church from a few families to a few thousand people by sitting on your hands. The pastors and church leaders we invited to that first—and subsequent—meetings were get-it-done types of guys. Alpha males. They chair meetings, set vision, worry over finances, recruit associates, plan special events, preach sermons, all while caring deeply about the needs of the people they serve.

So taking these pastors to a remote spot in the middle of nowhere made a lot of sense. Along with the fact that tucked into the mountains sat a rather unremarkable structure known as Sanso Cabin—home to Peter and Doris for one month every summer.

My newly formed venture, Leadership Network, consisted of three people: Fred Smith, Gayle Carpenter, and me. What we may have lacked in numbers and sophistication, we made up with passion and resourcefulness. For example, to get the pastors from the Denver airport to Estes Park, we rented three oversized passenger vans. Fred drove one. Gayle drove another and pressed her husband into service to drive the third. Gayle had helped the pastors arrange their flights so that they all arrived at the airport at approximately the same time, then led the caravan up the mountains and into Estes Park.

The plan was simple. Two days of Peter. I think we may

have given them a couple of hours off each afternoon, but I don't recall seeing any preachers riding horses or trying out the zip line. They couldn't get enough of Peter. Fred and I took turns moderating, but basically each session was Peter talking for about two hours to a completely spellbound audience, followed by a half hour or so of lively question and answer. Then we'd break for lunch or a snack and go right back at it.

The room in which we met was well-equipped with a podium and whiteboard, but Peter always chose to sit on a table, his legs dangling above the floor in an almost-child-like manner. I've attended my share of "professional development" seminars and other business-related conferences, and attendance dwindles as the day goes on. Not with Peter. The only time these guys weren't paying full attention to him was when they lowered their gaze, almost in unison, to their notebooks to record some pithy thought, of which there were many.

MANAGING THE CHURCH TO BE MORE CHURCH-LIKE

Though we never really announced a topic for the event or his specific sessions with the pastors, Peter basically translated his views of management into a language and context that pastors would understand. But as Peter always pointed out to them, "The function of management in a church is to make the church more church-like, not to make it more business-like." Years before mega-churches were criticized for being too market-driven and business-like, Peter anticipated that criticism and warned these pastors against abandoning their mission. He reminded them that their success is largely due to the fact that their churches were *pastoral*, meaning that they served individuals, understood their needs, and cared for their souls. He understood the tendency for institutions to gradually exist for themselves rather than for the people they serve and exhorted these men to never forget their true calling.

Years before mega-churches were criticized for being too market-driven and business-like, Peter anticipated that criticism and warned these pastors against abandoning their mission.

As was always the case with Peter, he had done his homework. For roughly thirty years he had taught courses in Claremont's Executive Management Program, and he noticed that he always had five or six pastors in attendance. As his interest in the nonprofit sector grew, he made it a point to get to know these pastors and stay in touch with them. So he knew enough about churches and their leaders to connect with the group we had gathered in Estes Park. But he also knew that these pastors were not your typical parish priest or shepherd to an average-sized congregation, so he asked as many questions as he answered. It was clear to me that Peter found himself in the midst of a unique type of leader representing churches unlike any he had ever encountered. He wanted to learn as much as he could about them.

I've also attended seminars and conferences where the "star" disappeared after his presentation, but Peter was so generous with his time. He could easily have slipped out after each session and retreated to his cabin to unwind or relax, but he stuck around and seemed to genuinely enjoy his interaction with these guys. During meals he rotated between tables so he could get to know each of these pastors better, and at break time he was always in the middle of a small group, listening as much as he spoke.

The response from the pastors was universal. One by one they would approach me during a break and mention something specific Peter had said that would directly influence their own work in the church. Randy Pope, the Atlanta pastor I mentioned earlier, summed up Peter's contribution this way:

Practically everything he said applied to my work as the pastor of a large church, but two things stand out. I had really been struggling with how to take people in

my church into greater depth and maturity of faith—
to go from sort of adding a little bit of church to their
lives to becoming mature followers of Christ. Peter
mentioned that he knew of only two organizations who
have successfully made a long-term difference in people.
Larger churches and Alcoholics Anonymous (AA). So I
decided to look into AA to see how they did it and if
we could borrow from them. I learned that there were
two keys to their success: accountability and a quali-
fied sponsor. So we began forming groups of five people
with an effective, equipped leader and it has literally
transformed our church. In fact, it has been so success-
ful that we have hundreds of pastors from all over the
world coming to us to learn how to do the same thing
in their churches. It has created a separate global min-
istry that we call Life on Life Ministries.

I also learned from Peter how to be the most effec-
tive leader possible. He said that very few people can do
three things well, or even two things well. Most people
can only do one thing really well, and once they iden-
tify that one thing and give themselves completely to it,
they are the people who make the biggest difference in
the world.

During one of the final sessions, I was standing in the back of the room, and a strong and uncharacteristic wave of emotion fell over me. Peter was up front with his sneakers swinging back and forth beneath the table he was sitting on. A select group of some of the nation's most talented and influential pastors and church leaders were so dialed in you could almost feel their eagerness to go back and put to work what they were learning. Peter paused with his enigmatic smile, and it hit me. It was happening! I left behind a business career to engage in something so much bigger, but there was always that doubt in the back of my mind. Would it amount to anything or would I just be writing checks to make me feel better? As I gazed out across the room, it was almost as if the Almighty himself was saying to me, "See? And this is just the beginning."

Peter paused with his enigmatic smile, and it hit me. It was happening! I left behind a business career to engage in something so much bigger.

I had to slip out of the room, I was so overcome with emotion. Thus began a series of similar meetings with Peter. We invited groups of pastors and other social sector leaders to spend two days with him. Thirty leaders at a time, five separate events. Peter taught in the mornings and afternoons, and we carefully arranged the groups so that Peter could have personal conversations with the leaders over meals. One hundred and fifty leaders in total poured their stories and management concerns onto Peter, who took it all in like the lifelong student he was. Peter learned by listening.

In my office I keep a framed picture that looks a bit like a high-school class's twentieth reunion photo: thirty-three men awkwardly posing and smiling into the camera against a backdrop of mountains. Sadly, some have passed on—men like Art DeKruyter who led one of the most dynamic and influential churches in the Chicago area, Christ Church of Oak Brook. David Hubbard, the former president of Fuller Seminary, the largest interdenominational seminary in the world. Ted Engstrom, former head of the international relief agency World Vision. These were senior statesmen who came and lended support to our efforts to nurture and encourage the younger pastors, and I miss their influence and friendship.

But as I look at that picture almost every day, I'm overwhelmed at what happened at that first meeting and several to follow. I see Leith Anderson, who led one of the largest churches in Minnesota, Wooddale Church, and now heads up the National Association of Evangelicals. Terry Fullam, who turned a small Episcopal congregation of a hundred or so in Darien, Connecticut, into a thriving church of more than a thousand members. Larry DeWitt who started a new church in Thousand Oaks, California, with six families and led it to become a dynamic congregation that now serves as a model for reaching the boomer generation.

And a middle-aged guy from Chicago in the back row with blond hair, a nice tan, and a white-hot intensity.

10

GO BIG OR GO HOME

"I bought one thousand, two hundred crates of tomatoes and got some of my loyal high-school kids together and we sold them door-to-door and actually raised several thousand dollars that way. In addition to that, those amazing high-school kids had part-time jobs and contributed out of their limited resources to help the church limp along."

—BILL HYBELS

IN THE 1970S, Bill Hybels, a college student from Kalamazoo, Michigan, was closing in on a degree at Trinity College north of Chicago and making plans to go into business. But one of his professors at the small Christian college challenged students to rethink everything they thought they knew about church. Hybels took up the challenge and signed on as a youth minister at a nearby church.

His Wednesday night meetings became so popular that

teenagers in neighboring suburbs would chip in to hire their school buses to take them to hear the un-churchlike music and Bible teachings that connected with their lives. Hybels might still be doing that save for the conviction that God wanted him to start a new kind of church, one specifically targeted to people who did not go to church.

A natural leader with an entrepreneurial gift, Hybels went door to door in his upscale suburban community. For several months, six days a week, eight hours a day, he knocked and began with one question: "Do you actively attend a local church?" If the answer was "Yes," he would thank that person for his or her time and move on to the next house. If the answer was "No," he then asked a follow-up question: "Could you tell me why you don't attend church?"

The majority said no, and of those, nearly 70 percent were very willing to express their exasperation and frustration with church. Hybels charted all their responses, but two stood out. First, they complained that the church always asked for money, and second, they observed that church was boring, routine, predictable, and "not relevant to my life."

Before he left, Hybels would always ask, "If there was a church in this community that did not go after your money, that talked about issues relevant to your life, that was creative and stimulating and practical and truthful, would you at all be interested in attending a church like that?" Many responded that they would.

A MEGA-CHURCH IS BORN

On October 12, 1975, Hybels opened the doors to a rented movie theater. The prior week he had invited all of those who responded favorably to his informal survey—close to a thousand—to join him for the very first service of Willow Creek Community Church. The theater seated one thousand and he was worried they wouldn't have enough room.

About one hundred and twenty-five—including his own family and friends—showed up.

"It was embarrassing," Hybels told Peter and me in one of our first meetings together. "But we kept at it. We concentrated on the Sunday morning service. We used drama, we used multimedia, we used quite a bit of music that did not sound much like church music. And I worked very hard on my sermons to make sure they touched life and were relevant."

He also paid attention to the first complaint people expressed. For the first six months, Hybels did away with one of the sacred cows of church: the offering. He never talked about money, but instead borrowed from his experience in wholesale produce (his father's business) to finance the church's first several months of ministry.

"I bought one thousand, two hundred crates of tomatoes and got some of my loyal high-school kids together and we sold them door-to-door and actually raised several thousand dollars that way," Hybels recalled. "In addition to that, those amazing high-school kids had part-time jobs and contributed out of their limited resources to help the church limp along."

Six months later, Willow Creek was up to five hundred people and Hybels finally relented. Just before delivering his sermon one Sunday morning, he brought up the subject of money for the first time: "Friends, we hope that after going six months without saying the word *dollar*, we've convinced you that we're not in this for financial gain. If some of you feel well-served enough in this church and want to make a contribution, there's an offering plate in the lobby. Just put whatever you want in it as you leave."

NOT YOUR TYPICAL PASTOR

I first met Hybels in the mid-1980s at the insistence of Harold and Robbie. According to them, he was just the type of church leader I was looking for: smart, entrepreneurial, and willing to use management principles to grow his church larger—much larger than what was the norm for most traditional churches. As I walked into his office, it was clear that this was not your typical pastor. He had the look of a business executive and an intensity that was palpable. As he shared with me some of his story, he stopped at one point and mentioned his sadness that in the process of moving out of rented facilities and into their own building, he had burned through one or two generations of managers.

> I first met Hybels in the mid-1980s. . . .
> He was just the type of church leader I was
> looking for: smart, entrepreneurial, and willing
> to use management principles to grow his
> church larger—much larger than what was
> the norm for most traditional churches.

I appreciated his candor, just as I appreciated his willingness to join us and a group of other church leaders in Estes Park. In fact, he loved the idea. I'll never forget seeing him sit quietly, almost smoldering, for two days. And then, out of the blue in one of the question-and-answer sessions he said, "I'm from Chicago, and I've got eight thousand people coming to my church, and I'm not sure what to do next."

The other people in the room almost fainted.

But that was just Hybels being who he was. He wasn't boasting; he just wasn't satisfied with eight thousand. He was relentless about getting bigger, not for the sake of numbers alone but for the sake of transformation—taking people from spiritual infancy to becoming fully devoted followers of Christ.

It was Hybels who coined the word "seekers" to describe those who did not attend church regularly but were curious about Christianity. That was his target, to use a marketing term, though even in the earliest days of Willow Creek he has been blessed with a core group of committed Christians to assist with teaching and nurturing the seekers. It was exactly what I had envisioned when I wondered what would happen if the church applied Peter's ideas in the management of their mission. Linda, who knows me better than anyone on the face of the earth, once said to me, "You're crazy about this guy aren't you?" And she was right. Bill Hybels is what Jim Collins calls a Level 5 Leader—leaders who possess the highest level of skills and capacity to achieve success, not for their own glory but for the good of the people they lead.

Today, twenty-four thousand people attend Willow Creek (when you combine those who attend the five regional campuses throughout metropolitan Chicago). A 748,940-square-foot church is the centerpiece of the 155-acre South Barrington campus that includes nearly four thousand parking spaces to accommodate the high volume of traffic for the three services every weekend.

The main auditorium seats 7,200 people on three levels

accessed by elevators and an escalator. Although there isn't a bad seat in the house, two large LED video screens offer "up close and personal" views of all that happens on stage, and what happens on stage is as captivating as it is inspiring: upbeat music provided by singers and a house band—all professional musicians; drama matching anything you'd see in a downtown theater; a dance troupe; and, true to Hybels's word, preaching that connects and is relevant to the lives of those in attendance.

Hybels once told me that he didn't think his real gift was preaching, but entrepreneurship. True, he could easily be the CEO of a Fortune 500 company, but his sermons, carefully crafted and grounded in Scripture, are as much a draw as the music and drama. So much so that attendance sometimes dips when he's traveling over a weekend and turns the task of preaching over to one of his very capable assistants.

THE HOPE OF THE WORLD

Willow Creek is big and beautiful, but it does not exist only for itself. Attempting to live out Hybels's belief that "the local church is the hope of the world," church members are encouraged to serve others. The original auditorium, built in 1981, now is used to minister to the area's Hispanic community. Over the past twenty years, the C.A.R.S. (Christian Auto

Repairmen Serving) ministry has provided reliable transportation to thousands of single moms. Its Care Center offers assistance in processing applications for food stamps, free health screening and health education services, free legal consultations, one-on-one employment counseling, and ESL classes — as well as a traditional food pantry stocked with fresh produce, meat, dairy products, and other items for families in need. The church also partners with a local organization to provide hot meals and a warm place to sleep for Chicago's homeless. Globally, Willow Creek offers short-term missions—trips that might include building churches in Chile or supporting those afflicted with HIV in Zambia. In all, more than seven thousand volunteers from Willow Creek serve on a regular basis.

At the risk of sounding like the guy on TV selling vegetable slicers . . . But wait, there's more! In the early days, Hybels told me that he would meet one on one with pastors who traveled from all over the world to learn from him. He simply couldn't do that and continue to lead his church, so in 1992 the Willow Creek Association (WCA) was formed to provide vision, training, and resources for church leaders. More than 8,000 member churches representing 90 denominations from 37 countries now belong to the WCA. Its annual Global Leadership Summit in 2012 reached 170,000 leaders—70,000 from the United States and 100,000 from 268 cities in 75 countries speaking 34 languages.

And this is just Willow Creek—one of more than 1,500 mega-churches in the United States that are similarly serving the needs of people in their communities and around the world. Churches like Redeemer Presbyterian Church that began in New York City in 1989 without a building and by 2006 emerged in a survey by Church Growth Today as the "16th most influential church in America." Or Life Church in Tulsa, Oklahoma. Crossroads Community Church in Cincinnati. Or Oak Hills Church in San Antonio. In virtually every major city in the United States you will find at least one mega-church— often several—led by entrepreneurial pastors and character- ized by actively engaged attendees who do more than just show up on Sunday morning.

> As Peter dug deeper into the phenomenon of the mega-church, his enthusiasm for what they were doing grew. He had seen the decline of the church in Western Europe and believed it contributed to the decline of European culture as well.

As Peter dug deeper into the phenomenon of the mega-church, his enthusiasm for what they were doing grew. He had seen the decline of the church in Western Europe and believed it contributed to the decline of European culture as well. Conversely, he once said of the United States, "If this country does not survive as a Christian nation, it will not survive." A fully functioning society needed people who were honest, behaved ethically, and cared for their neighbors, and Peter saw the mega-church nurturing those qualities in their adherents and subsequently in their communities. And they were doing so on a much larger scale than the traditional church that seemed mired in the noble mission of keeping its head above water.

Countless times he advised me to work with those pastors and churches who were willing to take chances for the sake of meeting the needs of people. In other words, my experience as an entrepreneur suited me better to come alongside churches with a grand vision rather than those who were just trying to survive.

This was pure Drucker: Build on islands of strength. Look for what's trying to happen. His counsel brought to mind the view of another consultant I once hired to speak at a conference for mega-church pastors. He explained to our assembled group that there were four categories of churches. The first he called *healthy*, and he suggested that in America approximately 15 percent of all churches were indeed healthy. The second he called *neurotic*. They have problems, but they don't know it. They say everything's fine when it's really not. He tagged these churches at about 40 percent of America's congregations. The next category he defined as *declining*. These were churches where healthy people were leaving because their needs were not being met, and in his view, 15 percent of America's churches were declining. Finally, there were those churches that he called *demised*. In these churches there are no healthy people and nothing to build on. As we like to say in Texas . . . stick a fork in 'em—they're dead.

When I shared this observation with Peter, he agreed that there was an enormous number of churches that are unhealthy and either declining or simply maintaining the status quo. "The way they decide what needs to be done is to do more of the things that don't work," he told me.

To Peter, the health and effectiveness of a church was closely linked to its uniqueness as an organization that answered to a higher calling. "The church must be a community—a community with a spiritual center, not a social center. The center is commandments and not good intentions. There is a difference between the church and a tennis club, and that is the spiritual commitment that only the church can offer. The church is not a service organization."

This was a theme Peter returned to often—the unique mission of the church to minister first to the spiritual needs of its adherents. He felt that without that spiritual dimension, the church loses its effectiveness. He pointed to the death of what he called "social Christianity" as an example of what happens when the church abandons its primary mission. Once, as we were discussing the various ways I might be able to serve the church, he offered me a profound bit of advice that I return to almost daily: "Never forget that the kingdom is not of this world and that you are not substituting for a labor union."

CUSTOMER SERVICE IN CHURCH?

One of the outcomes of our meetings between Peter and groups of pastors was that we began being contacted by seminaries. They wanted to know what we were teaching so that they might adjust their curricula used to train "traditional" pastors. In response, Leadership Network sponsored an extensive survey conducted of seminary-trained pastors. Carolyn Weese, a renowned church leadership expert, interviewed 105 pastors representing seven major evangelical seminaries to learn what seminaries did right and what they were not doing well.

What we learned was that seminaries did a good job of teaching potential pastors about things like church history, theology, and Greek and Hebrew. But they did a very poor job of preparing leaders. Here are some of the verbatim responses to the question, "What are seminaries not doing well?"

- Understanding culture
- Teaching leadership
- Teaching relational skills
- Extremely weak on the practical side of ministry
- Management skills
- Too much theory; not enough in the practical hands-on area
- Not globally connected
- Teaching vision for ministry
- Training in the use of modern media

In other words, seminaries were not producing leaders with the same skills being exhibited by the pastors of mega-churches, which helped to explain why so many traditional churches were in decline. As one of the respondents noted, "Our seminary graduates are being turned out into congregations with no vision for ministry and no capacity to mobilize their members to pursue an excellent agenda for ministry for Christ and to organize for such missions."

I think that's why Peter was so fascinated with people like Bill Hybels. He loved how these larger churches paid attention to the needs of their "customers" and adapted to meet those needs. He seemed fascinated that they were already applying principles of management and professional leadership to their work, something not always seen in religious organizations. (In fairness to seminaries, since we conducted our research in 1993, many seminaries have updated their approach to training future pastors.) Peter shouldn't have been surprised that this new breed of pastors was so open to his counsel. Just like me, many of these pastors were already Peter Drucker fans before I arranged for them to meet with him. Part of the professional development curriculum for all the department heads at Willow Creek includes a guided study of Peter's book *The Effective Executive*.

> I think that's why Peter was so fascinated with people like Bill Hybels. They were already applying principles of management and professional leadership to their work, something he had not always seen in religious organizations.

Peter also recognized that although the mega-churches shared the same mission of introducing the non-churched to the gospel and helping them grow into mature followers of Christ, they were not necessarily clones of each other. Or to put it another way, what works in suburban Chicago does not necessarily work in Southern California.

11

PURPOSEFUL INNOVATION

"I was basically doing what Peter had taught as being basic to any successful enterprise—know your customer and find out what your customer values."

—RICK WARREN

FIVE YEARS AFTER Bill Hybels began knocking on doors in the Midwest, a young man fresh out of seminary, along with his wife, packed everything they owned into a little U-Haul trailer and drove to their newly rented condo in Orange County, California. Both possessed a passionate desire to start a church that would be "a place where the hurting, the depressed, the confused can find love, acceptance, help, hope, forgiveness, and encouragement."

Two weeks after unpacking their trailer, Rick and Kay Warren welcomed one other couple into their condo for a Bible study. A few months later, on Easter Sunday, Saddleback Valley Community Church held its first public service with 205 people showing up at the auditorium of Laguna Hills High School. An ambitious yet practical visionary, Warren was determined not to pour money into a building until they reached ten thousand people in attendance, a commitment that led to something of a nomadic existence for this church. Since that first service at the high school, Saddleback (as it is commonly known) has used nearly eighty facilities.

NOT YOUR TYPICAL BAPTIST CHURCH

When I first met Warren, I instantly liked him. How can you not like a guy with an engaging smile who wraps nearly everyone he meets in a big, warm bear hug? His enthusiasm is almost childlike, and his humility immediately puts you at ease.

"People want to know my secrets of success," he once told me. "But the truth is, I've learned by doing, and I've learned more from my failures than from my successes."

When you drive past Willow Creek, you might mistake the campus for the global headquarters of a Fortune 500 company; when you pull into the parking lot of Saddleback, you're more likely to think Bible theme park. An interactive playground for children, created by a member who happens to be one of Disney's top theme-park designers, subtly teaches Bible stories, complete with a Jordan River and Red Sea that can be "parted" to demonstrate Moses's great miracle. Older kids have their own climbing rock wall, cutting-edge video games, and life-like reptiles to observe in the "Lizard Lounge." Saddleback's state-of-the-art student ministry center, "The Refinery," serves 2,500 young people every weekend and is considered the premier student ministry facility in the world.

The various names of Saddleback's age- and interest-specific ministries offer a glimpse into the church's innovative DNA: "Wildside," "Crave," "Fuel," "Edge," and "The Herd." This is clearly not your typical Baptist church, despite the fact that Warren is officially affiliated with the Southern Baptist Convention denomination.

When the congregation finally built its very own auditorium, it was a modest facility that seats 3,500. This means that Saddleback has to conduct six weekend services to handle the twenty thousand or so regular attendees. Whenever pastors like Hybels or Warren throw around numbers like that, critics sometime accuse them of being interested only in size. Nothing could be further from the truth. These church leaders have simply adopted an important Drucker principle: Good intentions are not enough; always measure the results of your efforts to make sure you are getting the most out of your investment of time and resources. "If you would come to visit Saddleback," Warren said, "you would see Peter's fingerprints all over it."

Like Hybels—and most other people who started churches

that grew to have thousands of active members—Warren first focused on his potential customers. For twelve weeks he pounded the pavement, knocking on doors, and listening to people explain why they didn't go to church. "I would just listen and write everything down they told me," Warren explained to me. "I was basically doing what Peter had taught as being basic to any successful enterprise—know your customer and find out what your customer values."

> These church leaders have simply adopted an important Drucker principle: Good intentions are not enough; always measure the results of your efforts to make sure you are getting the most out of your investment of time and resources.

Apparently, non-churchgoers on the West Coast have some needs similar to their counterparts in South Barrington, Illinois. Warren learned that the top two reasons people didn't attend church were boring, irrelevant sermons and constant pleas for money. But his interviews also revealed some differences. People in his community felt that churches were more like a private club or clique, and that they also worried about childcare.

"None of the reasons people didn't want to go to church were theological reasons," Warren discovered. "I didn't meet one person who said they didn't believe in God. They just didn't like to go to church."

So Warren had everything he needed to design a church that would meet the needs of a large customer base, allowing him to accomplish his mission of introducing people to God and helping them grow in their faith so that they, in turn, serve others. Here's what he told Peter and me about the launch of Saddleback:

> *I wrote an open letter to the whole community telling them I wanted to build a church for those who had given up on traditional church services. I listed the four complaints people had about church and explained how we would be different, and invited them to come and see for themselves on Easter Sunday. Then I recruited my little home Bible study group of about ten people and we hand-stamped and hand-addressed fifteen thousand letters and sent them out, and that's how Saddleback got started.*

A STEADY STREAM OF INNOVATION

Warren also credits Peter for helping him understand how to be an effective leader.

"It was Peter who taught me that leaders do not start with the question 'What do I want to do?'" he once told me. "Instead, great leaders always ask, 'What needs to be done?'"

When it comes to church, that distinction is important. In many ways, the last thing the world—or at least the U.S.—needs is another church. I suspect a lot of young men and now women coming out of seminary would like to start a church. That's the "What do I want to do?" question. By asking, "What needs to be done?" these mega-church pastors learned to pay attention to the needs within their communities and create churches very unlike the churches that may be doing a wonderful job with their congregations but have largely been ignored by those people we call the un-churched.

Saddleback and Willow Creek have been around now for the better part of three decades, more than long enough to have experienced the institutional atrophy that plague most start-up businesses. Several years ago, Lyle Schaller, a very wise and observant church-growth expert, suggested that churches go through five phases: birth, growth, stability, decline, and death. At the time he estimated that about 65 to 70 percent of all churches in America find themselves somewhere between stability and decline. Yet these large churches, and others like them, continue to grow and demonstrate the same level of enthusiasm and passion that they did in their idealistic youth. How do they do it?

In the 1970s, these types of churches were new and highly innovative. They experimented with different forms of music and different styles of worship. They reinvented the whole concept of church—what it looked like, the services it provided, and the people it targeted. However, yesterday's innovation can end up being today's status quo. As I've come to learn through my involvement with these larger churches, they never rest on their laurels but constantly monitor their effectiveness and are willing to try something new if the old ways aren't working. It's what separates a fad from what Peter called "purposeful innovation," which results from "analysis, systematic review, and hard work, and can be taught, replicated, and learned."

> As I've come to learn through my involvement with these larger churches, they never rest on their laurels. . . . It's what separates a fad from what Peter called "purposeful innovation."

From the very beginning of my relationship with Warren, I felt his greatest strength was as an ingenious systems thinker.

He could look at the big picture and see how things fit together. Once when Peter and I met with Warren, our discussion turned to the process of helping new converts grow and mature in their faith. Using the analogy of a baseball diamond, Warren described new believers as beginning at first base. The goal was to get them headed to maturity (second base), ministry (third base), and finally mission (home plate). He explained to Peter that Saddleback initially started special classes for new members, taught by older, more experienced Christians. But as they monitored these classes, it became apparent that the new members kept getting stranded on first base.

"So we tried something new," he explained to us. "We found that new believers actually grow faster when you put them with other new believers than when you put them with old believers. And when you put new believers together, they are much more action-oriented. The problem with most American churches is that they teach too much and don't do enough."

It is that same willingness to not only monitor results but have the courage to kill the sacred cow when it gets in the way that led Willow Creek recently to make massive changes in the way it disciples new believers. After the findings from a comprehensive survey of the congregation by a professional research firm came in, the team responsible for commissioning the survey was understandably nervous about presenting the results to the boss, Bill Hybels. In short, the survey revealed that all the activities designed to help people grow were not working. But after the presentation, Hybels scheduled a three-day meeting to go over the results with the church's senior leaders. Before diving into what might be devastating news for his colleagues who had invested so much in the work of the church, he reminded them that "facts are our friends."

INNOVATE FOR ACTION

When I started working with the pastors of large churches in 1984, there were approximately six hundred churches in America with an average weekly attendance of more than one thousand people. By 2012, their ranks had ballooned to more than six thousand. Peter once told me that the essential ingredient of success is a steady stream of innovation. The first act of innovation is hard enough for many people, but to follow with Act Two, Act Three, and beyond is more of a discipline than a gift. And it calls for those most vested in the organization to listen carefully to those they serve.

If Act One in the rise of large successful churches was the building of large campuses, Act Two is a phenomenon known as the "multi-site" church where instead of adding on to an existing building, churches establish "satellite" campuses to better serve their communities. Churches like Life

Church, based in Oklahoma City but with fifteen locations around the country. Or Mars Hill Church, based in Seattle but with sites in several states. You might call these churches high tech and high touch. The music is live and the pastoral care and small groups are all done by live human beings with lay backgrounds. The message, and only the message, is delivered via DVD by the pastor of the founding church. At Life Church, for example, each of the fifteen sites hear a powerful sermon delivered by one of the best preachers in the country, Craig Groeschel. This innovation in large churches comes partly from the recognition that ministry is about people, not buildings. In fact, today approximately 50 percent of all megachurches are multi-site.

And Act Three? Here's where it gets interesting. On Easter Sunday in 2012, Life Church (mentioned above) reported attendance of 71,000! But in 177 different worship events at their various sites. Which means that the average gathering of people at each service numbered "only" 401. Similarly, Mars Hill's average attendance at each Easter service was 479. The trend seems to be that as these churches scale up they are at the same time finding ways to build more intimacy. In other words, the next innovation in large churches might be small.

The subtext of Act Three might be the growth of the church into what I call second- and third-tier cities. Conventional wisdom in church circles suggests growth occurs primarily in big cities and their suburbs. The surprising trend is that expansive church campuses are cropping up in all types of locales. When Linda and I drive the twenty-five miles from our farm to Tyler, Texas, we pass five multi-site locations of larger, downtown churches.

> Thanks to Peter's influence, everything we do is aimed at action and results: How can we apply these ideas in a practical manner that will help the church transform society? We basically ask ourselves, "What is God doing now? How can we join? What's next?"

These are the kinds of things we do at Leadership Network: observe, learn, innovate, and then provide seed resources to what appears to be the next great thing waiting to happen in Christ's church. I have the privilege of walking about twelve feet across the hall from my office to meet with mega-church leaders in our Collaboration Center. Upwards of fifty times a year we bring pastors and church leaders to Dallas so that we can all learn from each other. We also facilitate "Leadership Communities"—groups of ten to twelve leaders who meet regularly to dream, create, and execute ideas into tangible results. Thanks to Peter's influence, everything we do is aimed at action and results: How can we apply these ideas in a practical manner that will help the church transform society? We basically ask ourselves, "What is God doing now? How can we join? What's next?" Recently, after speaking to a group we had brought together, Jim Collins handed me a note: "You have helped build the most sophisticated human enterprise in the world." And to that, I simply say, "Thank you, Peter."

From my experience in business and with churches, the natural tendency is for organizations to get "hardening of the arteries," become institutionalized, and focus more on the needs of the inside employees rather than adapting to the needs of a very quickly changing consumer base. Whether multi-site or a single facility, the key to the success of these mega-churches is their focus on the needs of people, not on maintaining an organization.

Peter was the perfect tonic for the "arteries" of these large churches.

And for mine as well.

12 MENTOR AND FRIEND

"It is through you and your friendship that I have attained in my old age a new and significant sphere of inspiration, of hope, of effectiveness: the mega-churches. You cannot possibly imagine how much this means and has meant to me, and how profoundly it has affected my life."

—PETER DRUCKER

IN 1997, *ATLANTIC Monthly* editor Jack Beatty, interviewed me for two hours for a book he was writing, *The World According to Peter Drucker*. This was pretty heady stuff, even for a Texan, and I confess to at least a small dose of hubris as I awaited the book's release. I was smart enough to realize that not all of my erudite observations would appear in the book, but two hours would certainly provide this world-class journalist with a fair amount of provocative material. When I finally got a chance to buy the book, I quickly paged through it, looking for my contribution, only to discover that all my pontificating on Peter had been reduced to a mere six words: "He's the brains, I'm the legs."

After I got over myself, I realized that those six words accurately captured our remarkable relationship. Peter passed along to me—and others—his vast knowledge of how the world works, and I applied that first to my business and then to the world of large churches. He challenged me with his thinking; I responded with a plan of action and, often with the help of others, executed it. I have given up thinking that any of my ideas are original or unique, for just about everything I know about running a business or nonprofit came from Peter. As I wrote earlier—and have said so many times—I have long since ceased trying to determine what thoughts are mine and which came from Peter.

Beatty noted that Peter "is a thinker, not an academic," and "above everything, he is a teacher." The distinction is more than semantic. Peter was all about results, coaching me to "write for action" as I embarked on my first book, *Halftime*. An obituary for Peter in *The Economist* contrasted him with "academic clones who produce papers on minute subjects in unreadable prose." His prolific writing was never intended to impress other professors but rather to be read by actual managers, giving them knowledge that will make their organizations more productive, which in turn contributes to a fully functioning society. His influence was widespread. By the 1980s, about three-quarters of American companies had adopted a decentralized model that Peter had championed in his 1946 book, *Concept of the Corporation.*

An obituary for Peter in *The Economist* contrasted him with "academic clones who produce papers on minute subjects in unreadable prose." His prolific writing was never intended to impress other professors but rather to be read by actual managers.

And, of course, he had taught me, especially as I was seeking wisdom about how to make the second half of my life as meaningful as possible. He possessed an amazing grasp of the context within which I was operating, adapting five basic questions he had developed for executives to my quest for significance:

- What is my business on earth?
- Who are my customers or those that I hope to serve?

- What are their values?
- What have been my results so far with that group of customers?
- What's my plan going forward?

I can honestly say that I never would have been able to enter into the new entrepreneurial domain for which I felt called without Peter's mentoring. I have always believed—and still do—that no one is indispensable. As we church people like to say sometimes, the Spirit moves as he chooses. Had Peter and I chosen some other entity into which we invested our resources, I'm confident that God would have raised up someone else to accomplish what he has through large, entrepreneurial churches. What I still find remarkable, however, is how our lives intersected and grew into something bigger than either of us could have imagined after that first meeting in his home in Claremont.

WHAT PETER DID FOR ME

Due entirely to Peter's stature, the business media not only took note of his work with mega-churches, but seemed genuinely intrigued that he spent so much time in a world unknown to them. In 2002, *Inc.* magazine published an article about how Peter had mentored me. In that article, which was given the appropriate title, "The Uber Mentor," I identified nine contributions that characterized Peter's influence on me as a mentor over the years.

1. *He defined the landscape for me.* From Peter, I saw four "horizons" that would guide my second-half efforts: the success-to-significance movement in midlife; the reality that people now have options—perhaps the biggest change of the Twentieth Century; that nonprofits need to be managed for results and performance, not just good intentions; and that organizational skills would be needed in order to grow large churches.

> Peter helped me understand that the "externally focused church" is a major social opportunity and that Leadership Network can help these churches become more effective in their communities.

2. *He defined the opportunities, the "white space"—what is needed now.* Peter helped me understand that the "externally focused church" is a major social opportunity and that Leadership Network can help these churches become more effective in their communities. The way we would do that would be to find and equip church

leaders willing to commit the time and effort to apply management and organizational skills to their work as pastors. We would then facilitate these churches teaching their large and growing peers.

3. *He helped me clarify my strengths and capacities.* I thought my strength was perseverance and money. Peter disagreed, telling me, "Your strength is to see the architectural structure of things."

4. *He identified the myths, the false paths, the incorrect assumptions of the "industry" within which I was working.* I think he knew the tendency of people working with nonprofits to think of themselves as the minor league where good intentions are enough. So he stressed the need to raise the standard of performance in my work with churches and others.

5. *He encouraged me to "go for it."* Peter was all about action. Don't just dream big; follow through. So where he showed me the need for effective leadership to build large churches, he also encouraged me to form (with Fred Smith's help) Leadership Network. When he helped me see the need for effective management of nonprofits, I joined with Frances Hesselbein to create the Drucker Foundation for Nonprofit Management. And when he helped me understand that I had a second career ahead

of me, I entered "halftime" and emerged with a book and an organization that has created a movement of second-half entrepreneurs who are transforming their communities. Without Peter's encouragement, those all would have remained dreams.

6. *He helped me sort out the right strategies.* I could have spun my wheels for years, had Peter not been at my side sharing his invaluable and practical wisdom. One of his most important contributions was to steer me away from denominations and seminaries and encourage me to focus exclusively on large church entrepreneurs.

7. *He affirmed results.* How can you not be motivated when Peter F. Drucker tells you (and repeats it in *Forbes*), "The pastoral mega-churches are surely the most important social phenomenon in American society in the last thirty years"? And also this: "Bob, you have accomplished far more than you think." Peter's affirmation was not given capriciously and always kept me focused on performance, which for me—and him—meant changed lives.

8. *He pointed out wasted effort.* Peter helped me to *stop* doing things. Or as he succinctly put it, "When the horse is dead, dismount." If something isn't working—or not working as robustly as it once did—I abandon what I'm doing and redirect the resources to more promising opportunities.

9. *He (gently) held me accountable.* Peter was very kind, yet direct, when he felt I needed a "course correction." Once he told me, "When you have no results, perhaps it's because you don't know how to do it," suggesting that I should either learn how to do it or hand it over to someone else. Peter kept me in a state of constant renewal.

Aside from the twelve apostles, I don't think anyone could have had a better mentor.

A few years ago, I asked my friend Joe Maciariello to try to make some sense out of the more than one hundred hours of taped transcripts of what came out of my regular meetings with Peter. Joe collaborated on at least two books with Peter, taught alongside him at Claremont, and is the coauthor of a foundational work, *Drucker's Lost Art of Management*. What Joe discovered, among other things, is that as a mentor Peter was not above learning from the person he was mentoring. Joe astutely observed that when our consultations moved into the arena of large churches, Peter knew little about the mega-church movement. So I became Peter's mentor on a phenomenon that was unfamiliar to him.

In his research into my relationship with Peter, Joe also had access to what I call the "artifacts" of our time together. For example, he found a copy of a work of art I commissioned to commemorate Peter's eightieth birthday. The elegantly framed piece was a marvelous graphic depiction of Peter created by a calligrapher and artist named Timothy Botts. It included a mosaic of interlacing hands, with three of Peter's famous questions inscribed across the bottom of the print: Who is the customer? What does the customer value? What is our business? When Peter saw it, he responded in his deep Austrian accent, "This is my life."

The guest list to this eightieth birthday party was itself a tribute to the many great lives Peter had touched: Andy Grove, co-founder and CEO of Intel; Mort Myerson, CEO of Electronic Data Systems and later Perot Business Systems; C. Gregg Petersmeyer, assistant to President George W. Bush and director of the Office of National Service; C. William Pollard, CEO of ServiceMaster Co.; James Osborne, national commander of the Salvation Army; and a host of other leaders from business, government, and the nonprofit sector. Frances Hesselbein, then the head of the Drucker Foundation and before that the head of Girl Scouts of the USA, helped me organize this memorable event in New York City. We called it "A Day with Peter F. Drucker: An 80th Birthday Celebration."

Within a few days of returning to Dallas, I received a letter from Peter, typed on his manual typewriter, complete with a hand-corrected typo. Peter was perhaps the most courteous man I've ever known, and I had grown accustomed to receiving similar notes of encouragement or appreciation. He never lost sight of the human side of every equation and took the time to recognize the contributions of others.

But this letter was different. In addition to thanking me for the birthday celebration that I had a hand in organizing, he revealed something that I still find incredibly humbling as it more or less confirmed Joe's view that in the best mentoring relationships, the mentoring flows in both directions. As the recipient of Peter's teaching and friendship, my life has been enriched beyond any measure I could have imagined. That the working out of my quest for a more significant life had any impact on Peter is a fitting illustration of what it means to be a life-long learner. This is a portion of that letter to me:

But above all, this is a letter of profound thanks for what you, Bob, have done for me and for the third "half" of my life—the last fifteen or so years. It is through you and your friendship that I have attained in my old age a new and significant sphere of inspiration, of hope, of effectiveness: the mega-churches. You cannot possibly imagine how much this means and has meant to me, and how profoundly it has affected my life. I owe you so very much for your generous willingness to allow me to take a small part in your tremendously important work—I cannot even begin to tell you what your confidence in me and your friendship has meant for me.

In warm and affectionate gratitude,
Peter Drucker

He could not have known then that his "third half" would continue for another fifteen years. Or that spurred along by his influence, large churches would continue to innovate, experiment, and change in order to do a more effective job of introducing people to God and nurturing their relationship with him. And that these churches would provide millions of hours of community service outside their own walls.

13 THE GOD QUESTION

"Mankind needs the return to spiritual values, for it needs compassion. It needs the deep experience that the Thou and the I are one, which all higher religions share."

—PETER DRUCKER

SO THE OBVIOUS question from those who know Peter as "the father of modern management," yet saw him hanging around the likes of Bill Hybels, Rick Warren, and me: "Was Peter a Christian?"

In an existential way, it really didn't matter to me, especially in the beginning of our relationship. I sought his counsel because I considered him to be the most trustworthy and brilliant thinker on the planet. Even before I met and then developed a friendship with Peter, I sensed from reading his books that he was a kindred spirit. Someone who valued the same things I valued. I never gave any thought to what religion, if any, he embraced even as he demonstrated a commitment to qualities such as honesty, fair play, compassion, and decency that are often traced to Judeo-Christian teaching. I sought Peter's counsel for my business, not my faith.

Although it is probably accurate to describe my own belief system as falling somewhere in the broad category of evangelical, I've never been all that comfortable with what is commonly referred to as "witnessing"—sharing my faith with others for the purpose of inviting them to embrace it themselves. I suspect part of that has to do with my somewhat introverted personality, but I've also always believed that the way I live says as much or more about my beliefs as my words do. Or to paraphrase St. Francis: "Preach the gospel at all times and when necessary use words."

So in the early years of our relationship, I probably said very little, if anything, about my Christian faith, nor did Peter reveal much about his own religious beliefs. And yet, when I began to hear a "still small voice" telling me it was time to make some changes in my life, it did not seem odd or uncomfortable to share this with Peter. To the contrary, it opened up a whole new landscape for both of us. Peter's interest in the nonprofit sector was prompted by his belief that the predominant need in our culture was to make our lives useful to ourselves and others, and that was precisely what I was trying to do.

By our third or fourth annual meeting, I felt we had developed enough of a relationship that I could talk about the other things that really mattered to me. The most important single thing in my life is to discover and honor the calling I'm responsible to God for. I was timid about even bringing up that subject, but as we were walking from his house, to go to Griswold's for lunch, I just asked him directly, "Peter, are you a Christian?"

"Well," he answered. "I'm a Kierkegaardian." He then explained that when he was eighteen he translated a Danish theologian named Søren Kierkegaard into German, and that experience had a profound impact on him. "But since that time, my religious side has been attenuated."

I listened and carried on as if I knew what he was talking about, which of course I did not. Later, with the help of an encyclopedia (this was pre-Google), I learned that Kierkegaard was a Danish Christian existentialist who was extremely cynical about the church but passionate about his faith as an autonomous individual. He railed against the state-sanctioned church that made it possible, in his words, for people to "become Christian without knowing what it means to be a Christian." And from a dictionary I learned that *attenuated* meant "stretched thin." It was the first time either of us had said anything about faith, but it opened the door for many subsequent conversations that ventured beyond my business interests and eventually led to my second-half career.

It was the first time either of us had said anything about faith, but it opened the door for many subsequent conversations that ventured beyond my business interests and eventually led to my second-half career.

Shortly after Ross, our only child, died in 1987, I was supposed to join four others on a small private plane out of Colorado. At the last minute, I decided to stay in Colorado an extra day. Tragically, that plane crashed, killing my four friends and leaving me devastated and feeling a bit vulnerable. So I went to see Peter, and his words pretty much sealed the deal for me in terms of how I would spend the rest of my life: "I know you are feeling a heightened sense of your own mortality right now, but the fact is, you have twenty-five years or more of your life yet to be lived, and they will be the best twenty-five years of your life." In other words, "Put your feet on the ground and get about your work."

As I began to explain my interest in working with pastors of large churches, it was clear that Peter was very much aware of their existence. In one of our consultations he pretty much crystalized my own thoughts:

> *It seems to me that you propose to exploit a unique opportunity. You have been talking of a "spiritual revival." You know that I'm a little reluctant to use such big words. But there is no doubt that the evangelicals are creating a new mode. They are making the church available to the modern world. And they are creating a church that fits the reality of our society in which a majority, or at least a leading minority, consists of highly educated and highly professional people who, at the same time, are increasingly conscious of the fact that they need more than this world, and more than material possessions, and more than worldly success. And the rapid growth and development of mega-churches creates the opportunity for developing an organization that assists pastors and leaders of these churches in learning how to lead, organize, and manage these organizations as their scale increases.*

He then went on to give me a lesson in church history, referring to both the First Great Awakening led by Jonathan Edwards and George Whitfield and the Second involving Lyman Beecher and Charles Finney. I remember thinking as he contrasted society's needs today with those during these historic spiritual movements, *For a management guy, he sure seems to know a lot about religion.* But as I had already observed, Peter was so much more than a "management guy." His curiosity led him to learn from all disciplines, and one of the best ways to learn, he once told me, is to teach. Peter taught everything from American history to Japanese art to statistics to, yes, religion.

Peter saw religion, properly lived out by adherents, as an ally to his vision for a fully functioning society. Commitment to the tenets of religious belief—Christian or otherwise— contributed to the ethical and moral health of individuals, communities, nations. In his 1957 book, *Landmarks of Tomorrow*, Peter wrote: "Society needs a return to spiritual values—not to offset the material but to make it fully productive . . . Mankind needs the return to spiritual values, for it needs compassion. It needs the deep experience that the Thou and the I are one, which all higher religions share."

Those looking to "Christianize" Peter might be inclined to point to his work with mega-church pastors as an indication of his personal beliefs. After all, why would a man who could make a lot more money consulting for other organizations devote so much time during the final twenty years of his life to

THE GOD QUESTION 149

the likes of Bill Hybels, Rick Warren, and me? It certainly is tempting to think that Peter singled out these large churches because he shared their evangelical Christian theology and doctrine, but that's not what attracted him to this subculture. This was just Peter being true to his own counsel: build on islands of strength. I am quite certain that if I asked him to help me work with one of the mainline denominations that was losing thousands of members annually, he would have politely declined.

> Why would a man who could make a lot more money consulting for other organizations devote so much time during the final twenty years of his life to the likes of Bill Hybels, Rick Warren, and me?

Whether or not he bought everything these mega-churches were selling, he was completely sold on their potential to have a positive and long-lasting influence on society. He saw into the future where these large churches could re-energize Christianity in this country and successfully address societal issues that neither the public nor private sectors had been able to resolve. He even went so far as to describe the mega-church as "the only organization that is actually working in our society."

To my knowledge, Peter never actually attended Willow Creek or Saddleback or any other of the large churches he influenced. He often accompanied Doris on Sundays to a small Episcopal church in Claremont. He possessed an impressive knowledge of the Old and New Testaments, often referring to specific passages and teachings when he spoke. He knew his Scripture well, encouraging me to be an even greater student of the Bible.

Once, when we were reflecting on how I made the transition from running my cable television company to working with mega-church leaders, we both agreed that it was a remarkable convergence of opportunity and need. Peter added, "I always maintain that the most important phrase in marketing is that wonderful phrase in the King James Version of the Bible, 'the fulness of time.' That's what happened with you—opportunity meets a prepared mind."

As I indicated earlier, it is not my intention to try and paint Peter as an evangelical Christian. He wasn't. As much as he respected and admired this particular slice of Christianity, he clearly observed and counseled them as an outsider. I have often described Peter as a faithful disciple who did not wear his faith on his sleeve. He was devoted to his local church and its leaders, but advised leaders of many religious traditions.

Shortly before he died, Peter granted an interview to Tom Ashbrook, host of the nationally syndicated radio program

On Point. It would turn out to be Peter's last interview. After nearly forty-five minutes of engaging dialogue, Ashford could not resist addressing the God question.

"Peter Drucker," he began. "I have a final question, and I hope you will humor me and not consider me too greedy. You have lived a life and focused intensely on life and how it's lived. Now you're ninety-five. What about an afterlife? What about God? How do you think about the transition that you are inevitably approaching?"

Peter did not hesitate.

"Well, I happen to be a very conventional, traditional Christian. Period! And I don't think about it. I am told! It's not my job to think about it. My job is to say, 'Yes sir!'"

"That must be very comforting," Ashbrook commented.

"It is, and I say every morning and every evening, 'Praise be to God for the beauty of his creation. Amen.'"

Peter went out of his way to not offend people, especially when it came to the subject of religion. He knew that anything he did that would lead people to say he was biased or cause people to think he favored a particular sect or subgroup would impede his main objective. For Peter did not think it was his job to spread the gospel.

His mission was to help save society.

14 SAVING SOCIETY

"It's up to us now.

—JOHN BACHMAN

THOSE WHO KNOW me well might describe me in a number of ways—both flattering and otherwise—but I rather doubt that anyone would consider me a pessimist. Gloom and doom has never been my game, and I generally try to avoid those who insist the world is on its way to perdition. While I think I have a realistic view of things, I tend to focus on success rather than failure. I prefer to be for, not against, something. I suspect that is a prerequisite for any entrepreneur, and the encouragement I received from Peter certainly amplified my sense that with a little work and the right strategies, you can achieve prodigious results.

But I must confess that an increasing sense of urgency has crept into my soul when it comes to releasing the latent energy of American Christianity. If anything, we need Peter's influence more than ever, and one area where I find hope is in the nonprofit arena. Peter once told me that the most effective organizations in the world are nonprofits. He believed that these organizations, if managed properly, could become the best avenues for meeting human needs and alleviating suffering. And in turn, these organizations could fulfill the needs of volunteers hungry for individual achievement and a sense of citizenship. I believe that's what he saw happening as he studied the mega-church. And in that sense, Peter found a vehicle that just might be capable of saving society. Or at least, working in tandem with other well-managed nonprofit organizations, it could contribute to a fully functioning society.

> Peter once told me that the most effective organizations in the world are nonprofits. He believed that these organizations, if managed properly, could become the best avenues for meeting human needs and alleviating suffering.

It was because of his enthusiastic embrace of the nonprofit community that Frances Hesselbein, John McNeice, Richard Schubert, and I created the Peter F. Drucker Foundation for Nonprofit Management in 1990. Knowing of Peter's reluctance to have his name attached to institutions, Frances, Dick, and I decided to sneak up on him one day at the venerable Griswold's Hotel. Armed with easels of newsprint and dozens of felt pens, we sketched and diagrammed and eventually put together what we felt was an honorable and efficient way to help nonprofits serve their constituencies more effectively, based on Peter's ideas.

When we presented him with our plan later that day, Peter predictably argued against using his name with this new foundation. Our work apparently in vain, we collectively shrugged our shoulders and headed off with Peter to his home. Halfway through dinner, as we continued to discuss the prospect of a foundation bearing Peter's name, Doris abruptly pronounced, "No, you will not do this." I was pretty much convinced that we had wasted our time.

But later that evening, we got a glimmer of hope. Kathleen, one of Peter's daughters, came up to me and quietly said: "Don't worry. This happens all the time. Keep moving forward with your plans and everything will be fine." The next day in the conference room at Griswold's, we were tweaking our design for the foundation when Peter walked in and affirmed Kathleen's prophetic assurance. "Everything's fine," he smiled. "Doris is on board, and so am I."

A MILLION ORGANIZATIONS WORKING TO SAVE SOCIETY

Frances, a remarkable leader in her own right, having just retired as CEO of the Girl Scouts, served for several years as the unpaid president and CEO of the Drucker Foundation. I became the founding chairman. Frances's summary of the foundation's purpose reflects Peter's confidence in what nonprofits could do for society if managed well: "We are dedicated to support one million social sector organizations sharing a vision of healthy children, strong families, adequate schools, decent neighborhoods—all embraced by the cohesive, inclusive community."

Since its inauspicious beginnings, the organization has trained more than 11,000 nonprofit leaders and provided facilitator training for 1,500 trainers who work with nonprofits. It has also been responsible for publishing thirteen books and four videos on leadership, management, innovation, and change for social sector leaders. In 2003, the foundation developed a documentary, *Peter F. Drucker: An Intellectual Journey*, which aired on CNBC. More recently—having first changed its name to Leader to Leader and now to the Frances Hesselbein Leadership Institute—the organization has branched out to work with corporate executives and fostered a fruitful relationship with the U.S. Army at West Point.

Meanwhile, I have kept my distance from politics, yet I did engage in one act of lobbying, and I did it on behalf of my friend Peter. A few years before Peter's death, Doris pulled me aside and said, "You know, Bob, Peter has three close friends:

Bob Buford, Bob Buford, and Bob Buford." Of course, Peter had many friends, but her observation held much credibility, if only because Doris is as straightforward a person as you'll ever meet. What began as a business relationship had truly developed into as close a friendship—save for that with my wife—as I will ever have.

So as a tribute not only to Peter's contribution to society, but to my own personal life as well, I decided to dip into what little political capital I had with my former governor who at the time was the forty-third president of the United States: George W. Bush. My idea was to ask him to consider awarding Peter the Presidential Medal of Freedom, which is the highest civilian award in the United States. I had learned that its recipients are always chosen by the president, and though I did not know Bush well, I knew him well enough for him to have given me a nickname: Bobby Boy. I guess that was his way of recalling the myriad names that a politician has to remember.

The trouble was, moniker or not, I did not have enough cachet—or the president's cell phone number—to be able to call him with my request. Fortunately, though, I had been in a small group in Dallas with Clay Johnson, President Bush's roommate at Yale and the man instrumental in helping the president select people for key appointments. So I contacted Clay and proposed that Peter be considered for the Medal of

Freedom. Evidently, the president agreed because Peter was among the twelve recipients of the medal in 2002.

Linda and I were honored to join Peter, his family, and a few other friends for the impressive ceremony in the White House. A number of Washington dignitaries attended, including Condoleeza Rice and Colin Powell, who watched from the front row. The president stood behind a podium and called each recipient to the small raised platform, and after a brief citation read by a military aide, he placed the medals around their necks: Hank Aaron, Bill Cosby, Placido Domingo, Katherine Graham, the World Health Organization's Dr. D. A. Henderson, author Irving Kristol, Nelson Mandela, Intel Corporation's Gordon Moore, Nancy Reagan, Fred "Mr. Rogers" Rogers, and A. M. Rosenthal.

In my humble opinion, Peter not only belonged in that august group, but towered over them. Though he walked with a cane, he did not accept the help offered him but strode up to the president and humbly bowed his head awaiting the medal. The president, knowing I had had a hand in this, winked at me and mouthed the words "Hi Bob" just before placing the ribbon around Peter's neck. Then, in a gesture likely unnoticed by many, President Bush gently patted my friend Peter on his shoulder.

This was the last long-distance plane trip Peter would take.

NOW IT'S YOUR TURN

On the night before the awards ceremony, I hosted an intimate dinner for Peter. The guest list was limited to Peter's family and a handful of friends—John Bachmann, managing partner of the financial services firm Edward Jones; Bill Pollard of Service-Master; and Frances Hesselbein. Peter had flown in earlier that day, taken a nap, and met briefly with me before we all gathered for dinner in a private dining room at Peter's hotel.

After the meal, we went around the table, giving everyone an opportunity to say something to Peter, and there was much congratulating and reminiscing. Peter expressed his gratitude to every one of us, and it was really a very warm, intimate meeting—perhaps more so than any other time I've been with Peter in a group.

> One of the last things Peter said before we all went our separate ways was that he felt there wasn't much left in him. That was when John Bachman concluded the evening with a statement that still haunts me, but in a good way: "Well, it's up to us now."

One of the last things Peter said before we all went our separate ways was that he felt there wasn't much left in him.

He was approaching his ninety-third year and though he was still writing, he knew that he simply did not have the energy or the time to continue at the nonstop pace he had maintained all of his professional life.

That was when John Bachman concluded the evening with a statement that still haunts me, but in a good way: "Well, it's up to us now."

And it is, for I am still an optimist at heart and believe that we can have the fully functioning society to which Peter devoted his life. It will not be easy, yet nothing of consequence is gained without sacrifice and struggle. It will take people of goodwill and generosity who are willing to invest their time, treasure, and talent into endeavors and enterprises committed to making their neighborhoods and communities better. Though I believe that the greatest hope for the world comes from the church, I also embrace Peter's wider vision of people from all walks of life—and faiths—working together to protect the world from tyranny by being good, honest, industrious contributors as parents, neighbors, workers, and leaders.

THE DRUCKER INSTITUTE

After that final meeting with Peter, my young associate Derek Bell and I attended a board meeting of what was then the Drucker Archives. As we sat around the conference table in the building that Bill Pollard, CEO of ServiceMaster, had funded in Peter's honor, we diagnosed whether or not Claremont Graduate University (CGU) was going to fully support the vision we had for taking Peter's ideas to new audiences in new ways. By then, the Drucker family was ready to determine whether the university would step up to the plate and champion Peter's legacy or whether they should move his archives to an institution such as the Wharton Business School or New York University that had expressed interest. I felt it my job and privilege to push this line of questioning forward by asking Robert Klitgaard, the then-president of CGU, a very poignant question using a line from Louis Jordan's popular song from the 1940s: "Is You Is, Or Is You Ain't My Baby?" In other words, could we count on CGU's partnership to perpetuate Peter's work and ideas?

The school's president affirmed our vision and encouraged us to dream about the idea of launching an institute rather than maintaining an archive since getting excited about an archive is a little more challenging—it sounds like a bunch of boxes in a storage unit. With that encouragement, one member of our gang asked, "Who is going to do this for us? We need someone to dedicate time and energy to making this happen." Without hesitation, I pointed to Derek and said, "He will." I knew that Derek would jump at the opportunity to be a part of a monumental challenge. With gusto he accepted the assignment and for the next eighteen months flew from Nashville, Tennessee, to Claremont, California, monthly to set the foundation for what would become the Drucker Institute.

The first important step in the transition from archive to institute occurred in May 2006. Under Derek's leadership, scores of leading Drucker-like thinkers and practitioners gathered in Claremont to help answer one question: What is Peter Drucker's legacy?

Attendees included Jim Collins, best-selling author of *Good to Great* and *Built to Last*; Paul H. O'Neill, former U.S. Secretary of the Treasury and former chairman of Alcoa; A. G. Lafley, then chairman and CEO of Procter & Gamble; Nobuhiro Iijima, CEO of the multibillion-dollar Yamazaki Baking Co.; and Masatoshi Ito, the founder and honorary chairman of the Ito-Yokado Group, Asia's largest retail chain.

This distinguished group's answer to the question was that Drucker's legacy amounted to much more than memories of the man or even his writing. Drucker's legacy, they said, is a collection of ideas and ideals that should be acted upon by future generations of leaders responsible for the companies and communities in which we work and live.

In due course, I became the founding chairman of an expanding board of advisors at the Drucker Institute, and

I've continued to support and guide a highly energetic staff led by Rick Wartzman, who had occupied senior editorial positions at *The Wall Street Journal* and *Los Angeles Times*, where his team won a Pulitzer Prize. Today, with a full-time staff based in Claremont, the Drucker Institute is acting on the vision laid out at that 2006 gathering. In striving to meet its mission of "strengthening organizations to strengthen society," the Institute runs a handful of key programs in which Peter's ideas and ideals have been turned into tools that are both practical and inspiring. Over the past six years, it has touched tens of thousands of lives.

> Today, with a full-time staff based in Claremont, the Drucker Institute is . . . striving to meet its mission of "strengthening organizations to strengthen society."

For corporations, the Institute provides customized C-suite workshops, or "Un-Workshops" as it calls them. (The name stems from the Institute's proven ability to provide understanding to get organizations unleashed.) These sessions build on years of work that the Institute has done with top executives— including P&G's A. G. Lafley, Jim Sinegal from Costco, Terry Lundgren from Macy's, and many others—spurring them to tackle some of their biggest challenges and move to action in a Drucker-like way.

For social-sector organizations, the Institute's work centers around the $100,000 Peter F. Drucker Award for Nonprofit Innovation. The Institute has turned the award application into a great teaching tool, with about 85 percent of applicants saying that the process of vying for the award prompts them "to explore additional opportunities for innovation in their work." Going forward, the Institute plans to expand how it disseminates knowledge through the application so that it can teach other core Drucker principles to the many hundreds of nonprofits that seek the award annually.

For government agencies, the Institute has launched a Drucker Playbook for the Public Sector—a series of twelve workshops in which municipal employees learn lessons on leadership and effectiveness drawn from Peter's teachings. The city of South Bend, Indiana, is now piloting the Playbook, with plans underway to offer the program to many of America's 280 other midsize cities over time.

In addition to these three core initiatives, the Institute ties Peter's timeless wisdom to what's happening in today's headlines, through a daily blog called *The Drucker Exchange*; a monthly radio podcast called *Drucker on the Dial*; and a biweekly column called *The Drucker Difference*, which Rick

Wartzman writes for *Time* magazine online. And, finally, the Institute still oversees Peter's archives—only now under the expert eye of a full-time professional archivist, who has greatly expanded the collection and made it digitally accessible.

More about all of these activities, as well as access to the Drucker Archives, can be found at www.druckerinstitute.com. (A final note: Proceeds from this book will be donated to the Institute so that it can continue to deepen its impact.)

Nearly thirty years ago, as a young business owner, I set a rather lofty goal for my net worth and with it a promise to give that exact amount away before I passed on from this life, which I estimated, with the help of the Cooper Institute and other assorted data, to occur at age seventy-five. (The Cooper Institute was founded by the Dean of Preventative Medicine, Dr. Kenneth Cooper, where I get an annual exam.) Peter's influence on just how I would give this money away was enormous. He once told me, "Your job is to release and direct the energy of others, not to supply it." Meaning, as I took it, the best way for me to achieve my mission of releasing the latent energy of American Christianity would be to fund efforts of the most innovative leaders to learn from each other and then make what they learn available to others. So what I have basically done for the last thirty years is get the smartest people doing church and put them in a room together to let them figure it out. My approach to philanthropy has been "a long obedience in the same direction," to borrow from Eugene Peterson, author and creator of the *The Message* translation of the Bible.

As I write this, I am seventy-four years old. Though I anticipate my seventy-fifth birthday and beyond with every intention of continuing to do what I do, inspired by the fact that Peter never retired, I thought a reckoning was in order. Am I making good on my promise? To my own amazement, I have surpassed my goal by about 40 percent, which has more to do with God's faithfulness than my generosity.

> I have reflected many times on these words of Peter to me: "The fruit of your work grows on other people's trees." It gave me permission to remain on the sidelines, offering whatever I could to those who could play the game far better than I could.

I have reflected many times on these words of Peter to me: "The fruit of your work grows on other people's trees." It gave me permission to remain on the sidelines, offering whatever I could to those who could play the game far better than I could. In fact, since his death in 2005, there has not been a day that I have not only thought of Peter but felt his continuing influence on my life. Peter once called me a troublemaker, referring to the Parable of the Sower. "You are not satisfied that what you are doing is enough," he told me. "The Parable of the Sower tells you that you have to produce results of at least four or five fold, if not a hundred fold. It's a very, very upsetting parable."

Upsetting, yes, but it has become the solution to another challenge Peter once gave me when he said an individual's mission statement ought to fit on the front of a T-shirt. I have chosen *100x* for my "shirt" because I believe it is my calling to become the "good soil" from which innovative, entrepreneurial church leaders can change the world. This essentially describes my approach to philanthropy, and I do not think I would have arrived at it without Peter's help.

Several years ago, a young man approached me with an idea that he felt would assist in the transformational growth of large churches. Out of respect for his privacy, that's as far as I will go toward identifying this project whose value I eventually came to see and subsequently provide the funding needed to turn an idea into reality. It worked, adding an inspiring dimension to the large church experience that it previously lacked. Peter was very much aware of my role in this innovation, and his succinct assessment of it helped me further understand my role in coming alongside others.

"He needed you for a long time. He doesn't need you anymore."

His tree and the fruit it is producing is doing just fine on its own now, which is the philanthropist's version of a gratifying return on investment.

The Bible says that each of us has a life task "prepared beforehand that we should walk in" (St. Paul in Ephesians 2:10). King David, in my favorite Psalm, declares:

> *For You formed my inward parts;*
> *You covered me in my mother's womb . . .*
> *I am fearfully and wonderfully made;*
> *Marvelous are Your works,*
> *And that my soul knows very well . . .*
> *When I was made in secret . . .*
> *Your eyes saw my substance, being yet unformed.*
> *And in Your book they all were written,*
> *The days fashioned for me,*
> *When as yet there were none of them. (Psalms 139:13–16)*

Each one of us has a life task coded into what I call our spiritual DNA. We don't have to acknowledge that code because God has granted us free will. It's up to us. The succinct way Shakespeare put it in *Hamlet* is: "To be or not to be, that is the question." The other big question is "how to?" For me it was never a question of whether or what to do, but "how to?" and Peter was instrumental in helping me answer that question by helping me understand my role in releasing the energy of others.

Another variation of his answer came to me in five unplanned encounters, all during one momentous week. In each case, I had long ago made a small investment of time or money in someone's life that provided a stepping stone for them to proceed with a task God had uniquely assigned them. Every one of these people had already been fully equipped. All they had needed was a shove. Someone needed to say, "You can do that," and to ask, "How can I help you?" This is what Peter did for me.

> I am convinced that many, if not most, serious believers at some level understand what their calling is, but that understanding may be buried under years of busyness and distraction. Yet, that suppressed sense of calling stays with them for years.

I am convinced that many, if not most, serious believers at some level understand what their calling is, but that understanding may be buried under years of busyness and distraction. Yet, that suppressed sense of calling stays with them for years, and as they leave church each Sunday, it follows them like an accusing shadow.

In explaining the Parable of the Sower, Jesus described our diversions in life as "the cares and concerns of the world and the deceitfulness of riches." The pressures to keep pushing for success are unrelenting and many—money, recognition, the best table in a five-star restaurant. People want their lives to count, but they lack two things. First of all, they lack clarity about their calling, which leads to courage and commitment. But they also need encouragement—someone to say, "You can do that. Let's talk about it until it becomes clear."

So now I am entering my third career as an "encourager." Trying to be for others what Peter was for me. From him I have learned that encouragement is a mix of:

- Permission—to be the person God designed you to be.
- Acknowledgement—a pat on the back that says, "You did it! Great work!"
- Applause—recognition in small but effective doses from people who actually care about you and genuinely understand the good work you've accomplished.
- Accountability—a critical element in converting "Good Intentions" to "Results and Performance."

Encouragement releases positive energy, lifts spirits, and makes the challenging and "impossible" seem possible. Usually, a little encouragement, delivered one-on-one and possibly invisible to the outside world, goes a long way.

A good way to sum this up is what I learned from my good friend Admiral Ed Allen, who was captain of one of the U.S. Navy's twelve aircraft carriers. He once expressed my role in this way: "The catapult is what makes the United States Navy work. It is virtually invisible but it gets sixty thousand pounds that is a fully loaded F-14 off the deck in about two hundred feet. You are not the carrier. You are not the plane. You are not the pilot. You are the catapult that gets the plane airborne."

> Everything Peter did—everything he wrote—came from his deep conviction that a fully functioning society was possible and that we all can play a role in making our world better and more humane.

Admiral Allen gave me a dramatic visual image that brings to mind the goals of all the ministries I'm involved in. It's what Leadership Network does for large church leaders, what my book *Halftime* does for high-capacity marketplace leaders in midlife, and what The Drucker Institute does for business, social sector, and public sector leaders. They are all catapults.

Peter was my catapult, and that is what I plan to continue to do for others. More important, this is something anyone can do. Everything Peter did—everything he wrote—came from his deep conviction that a fully functioning society was possible and that we all can play a role in making our world better and more humane. It may seem arrogant or outrageous that Peter Drucker and a Texas entrepreneur could conspire to change the world, but that's what we tried our best to do. Different in many ways, we both believed that there is a better way, a nobler goal, a higher calling for all of us. And that if we could even in a small way help mobilize churches to invite others to share in that calling, the world could indeed be transformed into something closer to what God designed.

I continue to be amazed when I hear reports that this is actually happening, and I invite you to join Peter and me to keep the conspiracy going.

EPILOGUE:
A CATALYST THAT FOSTERED A MOVEMENT

THE CHURCH GROWTH Movement began to lose its *mojo*. That's not exactly a scholarly word, but you get the point. After a promising start, it began to decline in the 1980s.

In 1956, Donald McGavran published a book entitled *The Bridges of God*. It looked at the strategies that led to an effective missionary process. The Church Growth Movement was birthed and those discussions and practices became mainstream within the church.

At that time, most churches didn't see the need to talk about or do much more than pray, sing, and preach. It might be hard to imagine, but fifty years ago we did not talk much about the mechanics of *doing* church. Many of these were helpful changes.

When I spoke at the fiftieth anniversary of the publication of McGavran's work in 2006, however, my presentation had a rather ominous title: "The Birth, Growth, and Death of the

Church Growth Movement." By 2006, few churches were talking about Church Growth experts. They were talking about—and listening to—key churches and their pastors. In a short amount of time, the influence moved from Church Growth specialists to local church pastors—key teaching churches and their pastors.

What you might not know is how that took place behind the scenes. You might not know how these teaching churches and their pastors became the new locus of learning for churches around the world—and how much of it happened because of Bob Buford, a quiet philanthropist in Texas, and his mentor, Peter Drucker.

Buford became wealthy in the cable television business and then decided to make a difference with his money. It was his influence that led to the rise of significant teaching churches, which has essentially replaced the Church Growth Movement and remapped evangelicalism and beyond.

ISLANDS OF STRENGTH

In the book *Reinventing American Protestantism*, University of Southern California professor Donald E. Miller writes about the rise of new movements like Calvary Chapel and the Vineyard. Their influence on today's churches is hard to understate. They did, as Miller explained, reinvent the church. Your church probably looks a lot more like Calvary Chapel than it does like your grandparents' church, even if you are in the same denomination.

As the Church Growth Movement was declining, new ideas like those of Calvary Chapel and Vineyard were on the rise. They changed the ways that churches worshipped and approached culture. Soon other churches took the new approach to worship and culture, and they started to add a new approach to leadership.

About that time, Bob Buford decided to find what he called "islands of strength" in the church and invest in them. The hope was that it would lead to an exponential return. The investment paid off.

Buford helped take a new approach to ministry, a reinvention of American Protestantism, and fused it with leadership savvy, the principles he learned from Peter Drucker.

Of course, Drucker was interested in the mega-church himself. He once told Forbes magazine that "pastoral mega-churches are surely the most important social phenomenon in American society in the last thirty years."

Drucker knew that millions of people had an opportunity to be connected to these churches. People were genuinely impacted by the community they found in healthy, growing churches—a community that was not available in the business arena.

The large church phenomenon has impacted North America—particularly the United States—in a significant way. The movement has impacted not just those who attend those churches, but the broader society as well, providing a different future, perhaps, than a secular European vision.

Together, Buford and Drucker made a huge impact on the direction of the church. Simply put, your church probably sings like a Calvary Chapel but is led like a Saddleback. Those two men are part of the reason why.

CATALYZING CHANGE AGENTS

About thirty years ago, Buford pioneered Leadership Network and began to influence the influencers. He invested his time to train the trainers. He sought to create learning communities that might foster mutual learning among high-capacity leaders. He did this early on with men like Bill Hybels, Rick Warren, and Robert Lewis.

Buford sought to find effective leaders who would teach others and then catalyze their skills. The end result was that leaders were pushed to a great capacity of leadership. Gifted pastors became effective leaders, resulting in stronger ministries. Their influence spread and, as a result, Buford's impact was multiplied.

Leadership Network never sought to be out in front. In fact, the goal was to fly under the radar of other groups. Instead, they sought to make the clients leaders and churches the stars, not the group, and certainly not Buford. Being behind the scenes was exactly the intended role—to be the platform and not the show.

These churches, with Buford in the background as a catalyst, began to slowly change a problem. Seminaries taught many pastors how to be students of Scripture (which is great) but not how to lead and manage churches. They often could teach and preach, but not lead their way out of a paper bag.

Buford helped bring about a movement—movements really—of churches that sought to have discerning leadership practices. Not surprisingly, they were effective and grew to the point that those movements and methods influenced thousands upon thousands of churches, probably including your own.

But that is what a catalyst does—in chemistry, a catalyst helps create a chemical reaction without being used up in the process. Then it does it again. And, as you read the history of Buford's ministry endeavors, you see a roadmap through the new influencers of church and ministry, all of whom were made more effective by the catalyst named Bob Buford.

MORE THAN MEETINGS

Buford did not just convene meetings. He funded the impact he desired. He did so selectively, however, only choosing investments that would create exponential returns. For example, he and Colorado billionaire Phil Anschutz financed the Burning Bush Fund. They took their catalyzing passion and combined it with strategic investment. Leaders like Mark Driscoll, Tim Keller, Larry Osborne, Greg Surratt, Neil Cole, and others involved their churches and ministries.

I was brought in as a facilitator on the second wave of the project. Seeing the names of those who were invited in the first wave, I was struck by how many were almost unknowns at the time but had since become national influencers.

Those were the "islands of strength" that Buford sought. He would find one and use his influence to build bridges to other "islands" so they could learn from one another. He made them better and helped them spread their story.

The end result is that churches are better led and more influential, all because of a person that, by design, stayed off stage and out of the limelight.

WHO TAKES THE CREDIT?

While the Church Growth Movement was declining and the contemporary church was emerging, Buford became a key catalyst in remapping the church's influence in the third millennium—all the while remaining relatively unknown.

In late 2013, I was speaking at a celebration of sorts for Leadership Network and the Halftime organization. I presented a chart that pointed to the growth in some sectors of the church. Later, I had that chart framed for Bob. Why? Because as a missiologist, I see his influence in that growth trend.

President Harry Truman is purported to have once said, "It is amazing what you can accomplish if you do not care who gets the credit." That epitomized Bob Buford's approach. He chose to catalyze his learning from Drucker and his fortune from cable, without much concern over the credit.

You may not have known Bob, but he probably influenced you and your church. More importantly, though, he's chosen to be a catalyst for kingdom impact—and I'm thankful for his passion and investment to that end.

Ed Stetzer, Ph.D.
President of LifeWay Research
www.edstetzer.com

MORE INSIGHTS FROM READERS AND FRIENDS OF PETER AND BOB

"Lots of people talk about playing a role in making the world a better place; *Drucker & Me* is a story about two individuals who actually have made the world a better place. Their willingness to listen, love, and learn from each other, and their focus on outcomes, created a platform that has contributed to a more fully functioning society."

Mike Regan
Chief of Relationship Development at TranzAct Technologies, Inc.

"For a half century, Peter Drucker was a guiding voice for both my father, who founded Yamazaki Baking Company in Japan in 1948, and then for me. It was Mr. Bob Buford who gave me the special opportunity to become Peter's last, and least, disciple. Bob's book *Drucker & Me* provides all the answers to the questions I had about Peter Drucker and his management theory. This book points to a new way and to a path for all human organizations to follow—business and nonprofit—that is fully functional and produces results. This book will be my second bible on management."

Nobuhiro Iijima
President and CEO of Yamazaki Baking Company, Tokyo, Japan

"Bob Buford's account of his journey with Peter Drucker provides an amazing insight into both fellow travelers that is well worth reading as a guide to being a leader and then doing something about it."

Richard F. Schubert

Chairman of the National Jobs Corps Association, Former President of the American Red Cross, and Cofounder of the Peter F. Drucker Foundation for Nonprofit Management

"Bob Buford faithfully and persistently models a life of doing for others what Peter Drucker did for him. His 'you can do it; how can I help?' servant's posture is a powerful mechanism for bringing out the very best in others and is a simple yet profound approach to accelerating impact and results. By serving as the 'catapult' and letting me be the 'plane,' Bob's fingerprints and core values are now embedded and living in the organizations I run. I'm now committed to doing for others what Bob Buford has done for me. Its contagious and multiplying. Thank you, Peter. Thank you Bob!"

Todd Wilson

Founder and CEO of Exponential

"Bob Buford invited me into his encounters with Peter Drucker, and my life has been influenced ever since. *Drucker & Me* now invites everyone into the same encounters and the joys of the journey."

Leith Anderson

President of the National Association of Evangelicals

"I am an absolute by-product of Bob Buford's relationship with Peter Drucker. I first met Bob in 1988 at a small gathering of pastors sponsored by Bob and spurred on by Drucker's coaching. As I look back two and half decades later, every major fruit of my work connects back to Bob. A better title for this book is 'Drucker, Buford & Me.'"

Randy Frazee

Senior Minister of Oak Hills Church and Author of
The Heart of the Story *and* **The Connecting Church**

"Being mentored by Peter Drucker was one of God's great gifts to my ministry. I remain indebted to Bob Buford for making that happen."

Bill Hybels

Founding Pastor of Willow Creek Community Church

"*Drucker & Me* is both a moving story and a genius handbook for creating a societal revolution for great good. Through the eyes of successful business leader and influential churchman Bob Buford, he describes in great detail twenty years of being mentored by the father of modern management, Peter Drucker. This brilliant book shows how Drucker and Buford became friends and successfully conspired through the American church and the social sector to create a better society. *Drucker & Me* is a rare book because the story will move you emotionally; while at the same time the pages will be dog-eared, reminding you of leadership principles you will never want to forget."

Dave Ferguson

Lead Pastor of Community Christian Church,
Visionary of the NewThing Network, and Author of
Finding Your Way Back to God

"In *Drucker & Me*, Bob Buford has introduced us to a Peter
Drucker few of us knew. Most think Drucker was all about
how to manage a business. That was never the case. He
was about people and organizations. His task was to make
effective organizations and help people achieve. His focus
on business was in large part because businesses, with
their financial information, provided a uniform way to
measure results. Yet as time passed and business became
hyper competitive with ever-growing emphasis on executive compensation and on the short-term, he became
increasingly disillusioned. It wasn't that sales, earnings,
and compensation didn't matter; they became the only
thing that mattered.

"About that time you came along with a different sort
of organization, one that was not about how to make more
money, but about social impact. It took Peter's core beliefs
and observations and applied them to perhaps the fast-
est growing organizations, namely mega-churches. Their
growth was testament to the needs and desires of a generation of people who found that their traditional church did
not meet.

"Bob's reflection in *Drucker & Me* shows a very different facet of Drucker and his work, emphasizing that
management is generic. In other words, the principles
are basically the same whether in government, business,
or the social sector. It starts with passionate leaders such
as Bill Hybels, Rick Warren, or Bob Buford.

"I just finished reading *Drucker & Me*. Once I got
started I could not put it down. Just as church leaders benefited from what Peter had to say, the application of Peter's
teachings to church leaders and business leaders who read
this book will learn from the modern church.

"As a fellow student of Peter, I was amused by Bob's observation, that he didn't know where Peter stops and he starts. I feel exactly the same way. I'm thankful for Bob performing a great service by showing us this aspect of Peter—both the man and his work."

John Bachmann
Senior Partner of Edward Jones

"*Drucker & Me* has brought together the BEST of Peter Drucker with the BEST of Bob Buford to bring out the BEST in everyone who reads this book. It happened to me and I promise it will happen to you. *Drucker & Me* is definitely one of the best books that I have ever read in my life."

Dr. Walt Kallestad
Senior Pastor of Community Church of Joy

"It is a little known story that Peter Drucker spent many hours in the last part of his life focused not on business but on social organizations. One of the leaders he mentored was Bob Buford, author of this book. It is not only a remembrance but also a call for social leaders to apply many of Peter's thoughts to their important work."

Dave Travis
*Chief Executive Officer/Chief Encouragement Officer
of Leadership Network*

"In *Drucker & Me*, Bob Buford gives us an inside look at the intriguing friendship between two influential men who together changed the course of the modern mega-church movement and its capacity to impact and redeem the world."

Steve Stroope
*Lead Pastor of Lake Pointe Church (Rockwall, TX)
and Author of* Tribal Church

"We forget that legends are real people too. Peter Drucker shaped a generation's views on business and entrepreneurship; Bob Buford transformed American Christianity. But here we see two legends as friends enjoying, supporting, and learning from each other."

Jeff Sanderfer
Founder and Master Teacher at
Acton MBA in Entrepreneurship

"While Peter Drucker transformed leaders around the globe with ground-breaking leadership principles, not many got to know Drucker the man. In this very personal book, Bob Buford shows that as great as Drucker's influence was as a management guru, he was an even greater friend and mentor. Thank you, Bob, for allowing us to drink from the same bottomless glass from which you drank firsthand."

David Delk and Patrick Morley
Authors and co-CEOs of Man in the Mirror

"The wisdom of Peter Drucker has had a profound influence upon many people. Some of us had the privilege of knowing him as both a friend and a mentor. This book reflects how Bob Buford benefited from such a relationship and then multiplied in the lives of others the wisdom he learned from Peter."

Bill Pollard
Chairman Emeritus of the ServiceMaster Company
and Board Member of the Drucker Institute

"Early in my ministry I learned what is at least a partial truth: He who does the work is not as important as he who multiplies the doers. Both Peter Drucker and Bob Buford are unique in that they have taken this a step further. They have left a legacy of multiplying multipliers. What Peter Drucker was to Bob Buford, Bob has been to countless pastors like myself—a multiplier through our lives. I have said countless times that few people, if any, have influenced today's church as significantly as Bob Buford. After reading *Drucker & Me* you will understand why and how he has done this—in large part because of an expert multiplier named Peter Drucker. I advise you to not just read this book but study it. It is filled with pearls of insight."

Randy Pope
Pastor of Perimeter Church (Atlanta)

"Bob Buford harnesses the story of his mentorship by Peter Drucker to convey to us, his readers, a measure of mentorship for our own lives. *Drucker & Me* will not only have you marveling at its front-row view of the unique friendship between these two extraordinary people. It will also leave you pondering in new and profound ways what your answer will be to Drucker's greatest question: 'What do you want to be remembered for?'"

Zach First
Managing Director of the Drucker Institute

"What a wonderful story of two pioneers of different backgrounds who conceived and implemented social entrepreneurship for the American Church and changed millions of lives."

Tom Luce
CEO of TWL Consulting and Chairman of the Board for National Math and Science Initiative

"*Drucker & Me* is a most unusual and inspirational book. It tells the story about Bob Buford's faithfulness to God's call on his life, which came early and came in season after he completed his obligations to his family. The book tells about Bob's vision and Drucker's active participation in helping Bob achieve the vision. Leadership Network, The Halftime Institute, and Bob's numerous publications are all devoted to helping people develop their gifts. This was a driving force in Drucker's life and work. The more than twenty-year collaboration between the two seems to me to have been preordained, and its richness can inspire each one of us to press on and try to make a positive difference in the lives of people. I urge you to read this book and take its message to heart!"

Joe Maciariello

Senior Fellow and Professor Emeritus,
The Peter F. Drucker and Masatoshi Ito Graduate
School of Management (Claremont, CA)

"I was captivated by the warmth and authenticity of Bob's description of his mentor relationship with Peter Drucker in *Drucker & Me.* Typical mentors offer lessons on the unwritten rules in the professional world, but great mentors focus on our 'whole' life including faith, relationships, and work. This is a 'whole life' book. I can testify that what Bob learned from Peter he passed on to others, including me: Bob catapulted the ministry I founded. To Bob, and now Peter, I am grateful."

Diane Paddison

Founder of 4word (www.4wordwomen.org), Author
of Work, Love, Pray, *and Chief Strategy Officer for*
Cassidy Turley

"*Drucker & Me* is the story of the friendship of Bob Buford and Peter Drucker—but it is much more than that. It is a real live case study of how Peter Drucker mentored and encouraged Bob Buford to do all that he's done the past thirty years. What I loved was not 'new' things about Drucker or his management principles but how someone I knew applied them. I was making notes in the margins about how those same principles applied to me and what I was doing. I absolutely LOVED this book. I love Bob Buford, and he's impacted my life so deeply—now I know where some of those ideas came from! Thank you, Bob."

Bob Roberts

Author of Bold As Love *and Pastor of*
Northwood Church (northwoodchurch.org)

"Millions know the work of management guru Peter Drucker and Bob Buford through Bob's best-selling books. But until now few have known the story of their long friendship and the profound influence it has had on the contemporary social landscape: It was their meeting of minds and hearts that launched the modern mega-church movement in the United States. This is a terrific read not only for the light it sheds on this transformative change in American religion, but also for its conviction that we can all be engaged in work that has meaning."

Bill Simon

Entrepreneur and Author of Living the Call:
An Introduction to the Lay Vocation

"Experiencing the last meeting between Bob Buford and Peter Drucker is something I will never forget—being in the same room as they said their goodbyes was a special gift. It has taken years of study and observation to understand the extent to which Peter and Bob have indeed changed the world in which we live. Bob, with whom I have shared tears, laughter, a mission to unleash the ideas found in Ephesians 2:10, and many memorable dinners has truly shaped my life. I am eternally grateful for all that Peter Drucker did for Bob Buford and even more grateful that Bob has done the same for me."

Derek Bell

President of Mosaic Trust and Associate of the Buford Foundation

"As one who reaped the benefit of a relationship with Peter Drucker through Bob's friendship, I can say you will not read a more heartfelt, accurate, and authoritative account of an extraordinary relationship."

Fred Smith

President of The Gathering

"As a young pastor I devoured Peter Drucker's management insights. Later, as the pastor of a so-called mega-church, I devoured everything Bob Buford and Leadership Network had to offer. Together they became my go-to for clarity and mentoring at the 30,000-foot level. In *Drucker & Me*, Bob pulls back the curtain to show how they fit together and to let readers benefit from meeting Peter Drucker—the man behind the insights so many of us have leaned on for years."

Larry Osborne

Author and Pastor of North Coast Church (Vista, CA)

"Bob represents to me what Peter Drucker was to him: a mentor, partner, and friend. The impact that Peter left on him made such an impact on the Halftime organization that I see Bob continuing to be my 'Peter Drucker'— being that persistent little voice, guiding me to become a better CEO, husband, and father. But, it isn't Bob's distinct and incredible leadership ability that stands out the most to me in *Drucker & Me*. It is the humility he daily exhibits as a servant of God. It is how he keeps the focus on God and the calling uniquely designed for him. I'm thankful Bob has allowed the world to see a little bit of the inner workings of his relationship with Peter Drucker. May we all strive for a similar impact on the kingdom."

Dean Niewolny
CEO, Halftime

"Bob Buford received much from Peter Drucker. I have received much from Bob as a mentor to me over the past fifteen years and for that I owe respect to Drucker as well. Bob has given his life to multiplication, and I have been blessed from it and passed that on to others. This is how it is meant to be. Be fruitful and multiply."

Neil Cole
Organic Church Planter, Founder of
Church Multiplication Associates, and Author of
Church Transfusion

"Friendships mark our lives, but rarely do we get to peek in on the lives of great men through the prism of friendship. *Drucker & Me* is an opportunity to do just that. Bob Buford provides us with a rare glimpse of an even rarer man, and graciously shares the fruits of his friendship. It is interesting and informative, a must-read for Drucker devotees, and a primer for those discovering him for the first time."

Ed Stetzer
President of LifeWay Research, www.edstetzer.com

"Many have been greatly inspired in leadership by Bob Buford and now he provides us with insights into one of the extraordinary people who inspired him."

Reverend Nicky Gumbel
Vicar of Holy Trinity Brompton and
Pioneer of the Alpha Course

"This rich, intimate journey inside the relationship between two world-changing men inspires me to not only have a wisdom source in my life but to offer it to younger leaders."

Lloyd Reeb
Author of Halftime for Couples

ACKNOWLEDGMENTS

I am grateful for the vision Byron Williamson and Worthy Publishers have shown for this story. Nearly three years ago my colleague Derek Bell sent our good friend, Professor Joe Maciariello, an iPod with more than ninety hours of recorded conversation between Peter Drucker and me and sometimes friends I had invited to come along. Joe digested that unpublished Drucker thought as only he could. After all, Joe was Peter Drucker's only coauthor. He came close to memorizing thousands of pages of content. Thank you, Joe, for your persistence. Everyone interested in Peter's ideas and wisdom should keep an eye out for Joe's next book to be published. The book will be the "how to" book that accompanies this story. Thank you, Lyn Cryderman, for shaping and bringing focus to my writing so that people will hopefully find it valuable.

To BJ Engle, the person who orders my days and keeps me between the lines. You contribute greatly to everything I do. Thank you.

And finally to you, the object of my work. Peter taught me years ago to guide and direct energy—not supply it—which means you have done all the heavy lifting. Thank you to all the pastors, church leaders, the exceptional people who are leaders, staff, and board members of Leadership Network and Halftime.

May your latent energy be transformed into active energy as our world is saved.

www.DRUCKERandME.com

has been created as a resource to add to the experience of Drucker & Me. Visit the web site to find an array of...

- tools to help you apply what you read about,
- never heard before audio,
- video from Bob and others,
- special insights on Bob's journey with Peter,
- and much more.

ABOUT THE AUTHOR

Bob Buford is a graduate of the University of Texas and the Owner/President Management Program at Harvard Business School. Until the sale of his company in July 1999, Bob Buford served as Chairman and CEO of Buford Television Inc., which began with a single ABC affiliate in Tyler, Texas, and grew into a network of cable systems across the country. In 1995 Buford wrote the bestseller *Halftime* (750,000+ copies sold), a book about how to deal with the second half of our lives. In 2004 he wrote *Finishing Well*, a compilation of inspiring interviews threaded with Buford's own experiences. In 1984 he founded Leadership Network (www.leadnet.org) to serve leaders of innovative churches as they enter the 21st century. In 1998, Bob launched Halftime (www.halftime.org), an initiative of Leadership Network that helps successful people to convert their faith into action and effective results. Shortly after Peter Drucker's death in 2005, Bob spearheaded the efforts to launch The Drucker Institute (www.druckerinstitute.com). You can find out more about Bob by signing up for his museletter at www.ACTIVEenergy.net. Bob lives in Dallas, Texas, with his wife, Linda.

HALF|TIME®

Success to Significance®

"Most people are over prepared for the first half of life and underprepared for the second half. And there's no university for the second half of life."

—Peter Drucker

WHAT ABOUT YOU?

Peter Drucker helped Bob Buford move from success to full-life significance—in a period of questions and thinking that Bob called "Halftime."

ARE YOU IN HALFTIME?

Call it "the university for your life's second half." Halftime is your chance to take stock, look forward, and chart a more conscious and meaningful course.

Start today to make your Halftime count:

Read *Halftime* the book
Attend the Halftime Institute

www.Halftime.org
855-2ND-HALF (855-263-4253)

Leadership✖Network
Ideas to Implementation to Impact

We believe in kingdom innovation.

We believe in kingdom innovators.

We don't create them.

Instead, we find them and
connect them to each other.

We move them from ideas to implementation to impact.

We share their stories with others to inspire, inform and
encourage the whole body of Christ to make a difference
in their community and around the world.

We help foster inovation movements that activate the church
to greater impact.

For the Glory of God's good name.

leadnet.org

My museletters are about my journey, especially what I'm seeing now, what I'm learning from what I'm seeing, and what action I'm taking based on what I'm learning. It's a book gathered from impressions along the way that I release in bite-size chapters every couple of weeks (delivered right to your inbox). Join my free subscription list at:

www.**ACTIVE**energy.net

My DNA has been shaped by three driving forces–God, Peter Drucker and the smart people around me (most of all Linda). This platform is meant to pass along some of the things I have learned on my journey from latent energy to active energy, from success to significance.

--Bob Buford

"Bob is in the middle of some fascinating conversations and ideas and I get the benefit of learning from it all through his museletters. Thank you, Bob. Keep them coming."

--museletter subscriber

WORTHY
PUBLISHING

IF YOU ENJOYED THIS BOOK, WILL YOU CONSIDER SHARING THE MESSAGE WITH OTHERS?

- Mention the book in a Facebook post, Twitter update, Pinterest pin, or blog post.

- Recommend this book to those in your small group, book club, workplace, and classes.

- Tweet "I recommend reading #druckerandme by @bobbuffordTX // @worthypub"

- Pick up a copy for someone you know who would be challenged and encouraged by this message.

- Write a book review online.

You can subscribe to Worthy Publishing's newsletter at worthypublishing.com.

WORTHY PUBLISHING FACEBOOK PAGE

WORTHY PUBLISHING WEBSITE

CPSIA information can be obtained
at www.ICGtesting.com
Printed in the USA
LVOW12s0114140816

500242LV00002B/5/P